gender roles
A CROSS-CULTURAL PERSPECTIVE

NATIONAL GEOGRAPHIC LEARNING | **WADSWORTH** CENGAGE Learning

Australia • Brazil • Japan • Korea • Mexico • Singapore • Spain • United Kingdom • United States

**Gender Roles:
A Cross Cultural Perspective**

Publisher: Monica Eckman

Acquiring Sponsoring Editor:
Kate Derrick

Project Manager: John Haley

Subject Matter Expert:
Wendy Perkins, Prince George's
Community College

Assistant Editor: Danielle Warchol

Editorial Assistant: Maggie Cross

Media Editor: Cara Douglass-Graff

Marketing Director:
Lindsey Richardson

Marketing Communications
Manager: Linda Yip

Content Project Manager:
Corinna Dibble

Design Director: Bruce Bond

Manufacturing Planner:
Mary Beth Hennebury

Rights Acquisition Specialist:
Alexandra Ricciardi

Production and composition:
Integra

Text and Cover Designer:
Bruce Bond

Cover Image: JennyLynn Fields/
National Geographic Image
Collection

For product information and technology assistance, contact us at
Cengage Learning Customer & Sales Support, 1-800-354-9706.

For permission to use material from this text or product,
submit all requests online at **www.cengage.com/permissions.**
Further permissions questions can be e-mailed to
permissionrequest@cengage.com.

Library of Congress Control Number: 2012933143

ISBN-13: 978-1-133-60359-7
ISBN-10: 1-133-60359-9

Wadsworth
20 Channel Center Street
Boston, MA 02210
USA

Cengage Learning is a leading provider of customized learning solutions with office locations around the globe, including Singapore, the United Kingdom, Australia, Mexico, Brazil and Japan. Locate your local office at **international.cengage.com/region**

Cengage Learning products are represented in Canada by Nelson Education, Ltd.

For your course and learning solutions, visit **www.cengage.com.**

Purchase any of our products at your local college store or at our preferred online store **www.cengagebrain.com.**

Instructors: Please visit **login.cengage.com** and log in to access instructor-specific resources.

Printed in Canada
1 2 3 4 5 6 7 15 16 14 13 12

Table *of* Contents

About the Series

Cengage Learning and National Geographic Learning are proud to present the *National Geographic Learning Reader Series*. This ground breaking series is brought to you through an exclusive partnership with the National Geographic Society, an organization that represents a tradition of amazing stories, exceptional research, first-hand accounts of exploration, rich content, and authentic materials.

The series brings learning to life by featuring compelling images, media, and text from National Geographic. Through this engaging content, students develop a clearer understanding of the world around them. Published in a variety of subject areas, the *National Geographic Learning Reader Series* connects key topics in each discipline to authentic examples and can be used in conjunction with most standard texts or online materials available for your courses.

How the reader works

Each article is focused on one topic relevant to the discipline. The introduction provides context to orient students and focus questions that suggest ideas to think about while reading the selection. Rich photography, compelling images, and pertinent maps are amply used to further enhance understanding of the selections. The chapter culminating section includes discussion questions to stimulate both in-class discussion and out-of-class work.

A premium eBook will accompany each reader and will provide access to the text online with a media library that may include images, videos, and other premium content specific to each individual discipline.

National Geographic Learning Readers are currently available in a variety of course areas, including Archeology, Architecture and Construction, Biological Anthropology, Biology, Earth Science, English Composition, Environmental Science, Geography, Geology, Meteorology, Oceanography, and Sustainability.

Few organizations present this world, its people, places, and precious resources in a more compelling way than National Geographic. Through this reader series we honor the mission and tradition of National Geographic Society: to inspire people to care about the planet.

The eleven articles in this National Geographic Course Reader present a wide range of global perspectives on the issue of gender, exploring social and cultural influences on male and female roles and behavior and how sometimes, those traditional influences can be overturned.

Three articles in the reader focus on traditionally male gender roles and the cultural and historical influences shaping them in three dramatically different social settings. These include:

"Mount Athos," in which Merle Severy explores the thousand-year-old history of a Greek mountainside where ancient monasteries welcome only men to lead austere lives in the pursuit of spiritual fulfillment."

Luis Marden's "Sicily the Three-Cornered," which takes readers to the mountainous island off the coast of Italy to observe the men who carry on seafaring traditions generation after generation.

and Robert R. Gilruth's "The Making of an Astronaut," documenting the grueling physical conditioning as well as the long hours of lectures and technical meetings that made up the training regimen for the Gemini Project astronauts.

Other articles featured in this reader explore traditional female roles. Among them are:

Karen E. Lange's "Himba: Consulting the Past, Divining the Future" which examines African women's tribal rituals that help them maintain a strong sense of community in the face of changes that threaten the tribe's survival;

and John M. Keshishian's "Anatomy of a Burmese Beauty Secret," investigating the custom practiced by the Padaung tribeswomen in Burma that requires them to mutilate their bodies to achieve cultural standards of beauty;

Several of the featured articles illustrate how women from ancient Egypt to the present day have filled social roles that challenged conventional notions of behavior. Such articles include:

Chip Brown's "The King Herself," which chronicles the successful reign of female pharaoh Hatshepsut, who ruled Egypt from 1479–1458 B.C.;

La Verne Bradley's "Women at Work," an article from 1943(?) documenting the surge of women in the workforce during World War II and their successful performance of a variety of jobs;

Marianne Alireza's "Women of Saudi Arabia" and Maynard Owen Williams's "The Turkish Republic Comes of Age," which focus on both the gains and failures of women to gain equal rights in these countries;

Alma Guillermoprieto's "Cholitas Fight Back!" chronicling native Aymara women dressed in traditional costumes who face off against each other in the wrestling ring; and Tina Rosenberg's "Necessary Angels" that tells of the successes of female village health care workers in India.

Accompanying each article is a summary headnote, a bulleted list of points to think about when reading the article, and a set each of discussion questions, writing activities, and collaborative activities that will help you explore in more depth the important gender issues that this reader addresses.

THE KING HERSELF

This article profiles Hatshepsut, who ruled Egypt from 1479–1458 B.C. The author explains how archaeologists and historians pieced together the story of this extraordinary ruler after discovering her mummy and other artifacts from her reign.

As you read "The King Herself," you should consider the following questions:

- How were Hatshepsut's remains discovered?
- What do her artifacts tell us about her reign?
- What traditions did she break in order to successfully rule?
- How and why did she try to preserve her legacy?

Abandoning the queenly attire of a regent, Hatshepsut came to adopt the classic regalia of a king. She wears the royal headcloth of the pharaoh, yet softly rounded breasts and a delicate chin subtly suggest her female gender. As a sphinx, she displays the unmistakably male symbols of a lion's mane and a pharaoh's false beard.

THE KING HERSELF

Photographs by Kenneth Garrett

WHAT MOTIVATED HATSHEPSUT TO RULE ANCIENT EGYPT AS A MAN WHILE HER STEPSON STOOD IN THE SHADOWS?

HER MUMMY, AND HER TRUE STORY, HAVE COME TO LIGHT.

There was something strangely touching about her fingertips. Everywhere else about her person all human grace had vanished. The raveled linen around her neck looked like a fashion statement gone horribly awry. Her mouth, with the upper lip shelved over the lower, was a gruesome crimp. (She came from a famous lineage of overbites.) Her eye sockets were packed with blind black resin, her nostrils unbecomingly plugged with tight rolls of cloth. Her left ear had sunk into the flesh on the side of her skull, and her head was almost completely without hair.

I leaned toward the open display case in Cairo's Egyptian Museum and gazed at what in all likelihood is the body of the female pharaoh Hatshepsut, the extraordinary woman who ruled Egypt from 1479 to 1458 B.C. and is famous today less for her reign during the golden age of Egypt's 18th dynasty than for having the audacity to portray herself as a man. There was no beguiling myrrh perfume in the air, only some sharp and sour smell that seemed minted during the many centuries she had spent in a limestone cave. It was hard to square this prostrate thing with the great ruler who lived so

To look upon her was more beautiful than anything.

long ago and of whom it was written, "To look upon her was more beautiful than anything." The only human touch was in the bone shine of her nailless fingertips where the mummified flesh had shrunk back, creating the illusion of a manicure and evoking not just our primordial vanity but our tenuous intimacies, our brief and passing feel for the world.

The discovery of Hatshepsut's lost mummy made headlines two summers ago, but the full story unfolded slowly, in increments, a forensic drama more along the lines of *CSI* than *Raiders of the Lost Ark*. Indeed the search for Hatshepsut showed the extent to which the trowels and brushes of archaeology's traditional toolbox have been supplemented by CT scanners and DNA gradient thermocyclers.

In 1903 the renowned archaeologist Howard Carter had found Hatshepsut's sarcophagus in the 20th tomb discovered in the Valley of the Kings—KV20. The sarcophagus, one of three Hatshepsut had prepared,

Adapted from "The King Herself" by Chip Brown: National Geographic Magazine, April 2009.

WOMEN WHO RULED AS KINGS

A pharaoh was meant to be both man and god, but a few women broke with that tradition. Only Hatshepsut enjoyed a long, prosperous reign, taking her place among notable male pharaohs.

Female pharaohs in red

was empty. Scholars did not know where her mummy was or whether it had even survived the campaign to eradicate the record of her rule during the reign of her co-regent and ultimate successor, Thutmose III, when almost all the images of her as king were systematically chiseled off temples, monuments, and obelisks. The search that seems to have finally solved the mystery was launched in 2005 by Zahi Hawass, head of the Egyptian Mummy Project and secretary general of the Supreme Council of Antiquities. Hawass and a team of scientists zeroed in on a mummy they called KV60a, which had been discovered more than a century earlier but wasn't thought significant enough to remove from the floor of a minor tomb in the Valley of the Kings. KV60a had been cruising eternity without even the hospitality of a coffin, much less a retinue of figurines to perform royal chores. She had nothing to wear, either—no headdress, no jewelry, no gold sandals or gold toe and finger coverings, none of the treasures that had been provided the pharaoh Tutankhamun, who was a pip-squeak of a king compared with Hatshepsut.

And even with all the high-tech methods used to crack one of Egypt's most notable missing person cases, if it had not been for the serendipitous discovery of a tooth, KV60a might still be lying alone in the dark, her royal name and status unacknowledged. Today she is enshrined in one of the two Royal Mummy Rooms at the Egyptian Museum, with plaques in Arabic and English proclaiming her to be Hatshepsut, the King Herself, reunited at long last with her extended family of fellow New Kingdom pharaohs.

Given the oblivion that befell Hatshepsut, it's hard to think of a pharaoh whose hopes of being remembered are more poignant. She seems to have been more afraid of anonymity than of death. She was one of the greatest builders in one of the greatest Egyptian dynasties. She raised and renovated temples and shrines from the Sinai to Nubia. The four granite obelisks she erected at the vast temple of the great god Amun at Karnak were among the most magnificent ever constructed. She commissioned hundreds of statues of herself and left accounts in stone of her lineage, her titles, her history, both real and concocted, even her thoughts and hopes, which at times she confided with uncommon candor. Expressions of worry Hatshepsut inscribed on one of her obelisks at Karnak still resonate with an almost charming insecurity: "Now my heart turns this way and that, as I think what the people will say. Those who see my monuments in years to come, and who shall speak of what I have done."

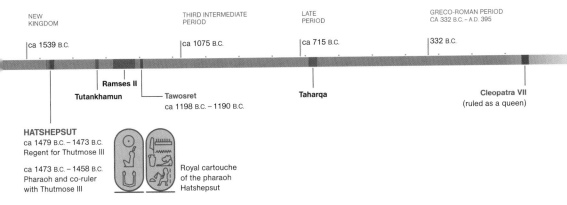

NEW
KINGDOM

THIRD INTERMEDIATE
PERIOD

LATE
PERIOD

GRECO-ROMAN PERIOD
CA 332 B.C. – A.D. 395

ca 1539 B.C.

ca 1075 B.C.

ca 715 B.C.

332 B.C.

Ramses II

Tutankhamun

Tawosret
ca 1198 B.C. – 1190 B.C.

Taharqa

Cleopatra VII
(ruled as a queen)

HATSHEPSUT
ca 1479 B.C. – 1473 B.C.
Regent for Thutmose III

ca 1473 B.C. – 1458 B.C.
Pharaoh and co-ruler
with Thutmose III

Royal cartouche
of the pharaoh
Hatshepsut

Many uncertainties plague the early history of the New Kingdom, but it's clear that when Hatshepsut was born, Egyptian power was waxing. Her possible grandfather Ahmose, founder of the 18th dynasty, had driven out the formidable Hyksos invaders who had occupied the northern part of the Nile Valley for two centuries. When Ahmose's son Amenhotep I did not produce a son who lived to succeed him, a redoubtable general known as Thutmose is believed to have been brought into the royal line since he had married a princess.

Hatshepsut was the oldest daughter of Thutmose and his Great Royal Wife, Queen Ahmose, likely a close relative of King Ahmose. But Thutmose also had a son by another queen, and this son, Thutmose II, inherited the crown when his father "rested from life." Adhering to a common method of fortifying the royal lineage—and with none of our modern-day qualms about sleeping with your sister—Thutmose II and Hatshepsut married. They produced one daughter; a minor wife, Isis, would give Thutmose the male heir that Hatshepsut was unable to provide.

Thutmose II did not rule for long, and when he was ushered into the afterlife by what CT scans 3,500 years later would suggest was heart disease, his heir, Thutmose III, was still a young boy. In time-honored fashion, Hatshepsut assumed effective control as the young pharaoh's queen regent.

So began one of the most intriguing periods of ancient Egyptian history.

At first, Hatshepsut acted on her stepson's behalf, careful to respect the conventions under which previous queens had handled political affairs while juvenile offspring learned the ropes. But before long, signs emerged that Hatshepsut's regency would be different. Early reliefs show her performing kingly functions such as making offerings to the gods and ordering up obelisks from red granite quarries at Aswan. After just a few years she had assumed the role of "king" of Egypt, supreme power in the land. Her stepson—who by then may have been fully capable of assuming the throne—was relegated to second-in-command. Hatshepsut proceeded to rule for a total of 21 years.

What induced Hatshepsut to break so radically with the traditional role of queen regent? A social or military crisis? Dynastic politics? Divine injunctions from Amun? A thirst for power? "There was something impelling Hatshepsut to change the way she portrayed herself on public monuments, but we don't know what it is," says Peter Dorman, a noted Egyptologist and president of the American University of Beirut. "One of the hardest things to guess is her motive."

Bloodlines may have had something to do with it. On a cenotaph at the sandstone quarries of Gebel el Silsila, her chief steward and architect Senenmut refers to her as "the king's first-born daughter," a distinction that accents her lineage as the senior heir of Thutmose I rather than as the chief royal wife of Thutmose II. Remember, Hatshepsut was a true blue blood, related to the pharaoh Ahmose, while her husband-brother was the offspring of an adopted king. The Egyptians believed in the divinity of the pharaoh; only Hatshepsut, not her stepson, had a biological link to divine royalty.

Still, there was the small matter of gender. The kingship was meant to be passed down from father to son, not daughter; religious belief dictated that the king's role could not be adequately carried out by a woman. Getting over this hurdle must have taken great shrewdness from the female king. When her husband died, Hatshepsut's preferred title was not King's Wife, but God's Wife of Amun, a designation some believe paved her way to the throne.

Hatshepsut never made a secret of her sex in texts; her inscriptions frequently employed feminine endings. But in the early going, she seemed to be looking for ways to synthesize the images of queen and king, as if a visual compromise might resolve the paradox of a female sovereign. In one seated red granite statue, Hatshepsut is shown with the unmistakable body of a woman but with the striped *nemes* headdress and uraeus cobra, symbols of a king. In some temple reliefs, Hatshepsut is dressed in a traditional restrictive ankle-length gown but with her feet wide apart in the striding pose of the king.

As the years went on, she seems to have decided it was easier to sidestep the issue of gender altogether. She had herself depicted solely as a male king, in the pharaoh's headdress, the pharaoh's *shendyt* kilt, and the pharaoh's false beard—without any female traits. Many of her statues, images, and texts seem part of a carefully calibrated media campaign to bolster the legitimacy of her reign as king—and rationalize her transgression. In reliefs at Hatshepsut's mortuary temple, she spun a fable of her accession as the fulfillment of a divine plan and declared that her father, Thutmose I, not only intended her to be king but also was able to attend her coronation. In the panels the great god Amun is shown appearing before Hatshepsut's mother disguised as Thutmose I. He commands Khnum, the ram-headed god of creation who models the clay of mankind on his potter's wheel: "Go, to fashion her better than all gods; shape for me, this my daughter, whom I have begotten."

Unlike most contractors, Khnum gets right to work, replying: "Her form shall be more exalted than the gods, in her great dignity of King...."

On Khnum's potter's wheel, little Hatshepsut is depicted unmistakably as a boy.

Exactly who was the intended audience for such propaganda is still disputed. It's hard to imagine Hatshepsut needed to shore up her legitimacy with powerful allies like the high priests of Amun or members of the elite such as Senenmut. Who, then, was she pitching her story to? The gods? The future? *National Geographic?*

One answer may be found in Hatshepsut's references to the lapwing, a common Nile marsh bird known to ancient Egyptians as *rekhyt*. In hieroglyphic texts the word "rekhyt" is usually translated as "the common people." It occurs frequently in New Kingdom inscriptions, but a few years ago Kenneth Griffin, now at Swansea University in Wales, noticed that Hatshepsut made greater use of the phrase than other 18th-dynasty pharaohs.

> The Egyptians believed in the divinity of the pharaoh; only Hatshepsut, not her stepson, had a biological link to divine royalty.

"Her inscriptions seemed to show a personal association with the rekhyt which at this stage is unrivaled," he says. Hatshepsut often spoke possessively of "my rekhyt" and asked for the approval of the rekhyt—as if the unusual ruler were a closet populist. When Hatshepsut's heart flutters this way and that as she wonders what "the people" will say, the people she may have had in mind were the ones as common as lapwings on the Nile, the rekhyt.

After her death, around 1458 B.C., her stepson went on to secure his destiny as one of the great pharaohs in Egyptian history. Thutmose III was a monument maker like his stepmother but also a warrior without peer, the so-called Napoleon of ancient Egypt. In a 19-year span he led 17 military campaigns in the Levant, including a victory against the Canaanites at Megiddo in present-day Israel that is still taught in military academies. He had a flock of wives, one of whom bore his successor, Amenhotep II. Thutmose III also found time to introduce the chicken to the Egyptian dinner table.

In the latter part of his life, when other men might be content to reminisce about bygone adventures, Thutmose III appears to have taken up another pastime. He decided to methodically wipe his stepmother, the king, out of history.

Historians long cast Hatshepsut in the role of evil stepmother to the young Thutmose III. The evidence of her supposed cruelty was the payback she posthumously received when her stepson had her monuments attacked and her kingly name erased from public memorials. Indeed, Thutmose III did as thorough a job smiting the iconography of King Hatshepsut as he had whacking the Canaanites at Megiddo. At Karnak her image and cartouche, or name symbol, were chiseled off shrine walls; the texts on her obelisks were covered with stone (which had the unintended effect of keeping them in pristine condition).

At Deir el Bahri, the site of her most spectacular architectural achievement, her statues were smashed and thrown into a pit in front of her mortuary temple. Known as Djeser Djeseru, holy of holies, on the west bank of the Nile across from modern Luxor, the temple is set against a bay of lion-colored cliffs that frame the tawny temple stones the way the nemes frames a pharaoh's face. With its three tiers, its porticoes, its spacious ramp-linked terraces, its now vanished sphinx-lined causeway and T-shaped papyrus pools and shade-casting myrrh trees, Djeser Djeseru is among the most glorious temples ever built. It was designed (perhaps by Senenmut) to be the center of Hatshepsut's cult.

Images of her as queen were left undisturbed, but wherever she had proclaimed herself king, the workers of her stepson followed with their chisels, the vandalism careful and precise. "The destruction was not an emotional decision; it was a political decision," says Zbigniew Szafrański, the director of the Polish archaeological mission to Egypt that has been working at Hatshepsut's mortuary temple since 1961.

By the time excavators cleared the debris from the mostly buried temple in the late 1890s, the mystery of Hatshepsut had been refined: What kind of ruler was she? The answer seemed self-evident to a number of Egyptologists quick to embrace the idea that Thutmose III had attacked Hatshepsut's memory as revenge for her shameless usurpation of his royal power. William C. Hayes, the curator of Egyptian art at the Metropolitan Museum of Art and a principal at the Deir el Bahri excavations in the 1920s and '30s, wrote in 1953: "It was not long…before this vain, ambitious, and unscrupulous woman showed herself in her true colors."

When archaeologists discovered evidence in the 1960s indicating that the banishment of King Hatshepsut had begun at least 20 years after her death, the soap opera of a hot-headed stepson wreaking *(Continued on page 12)*

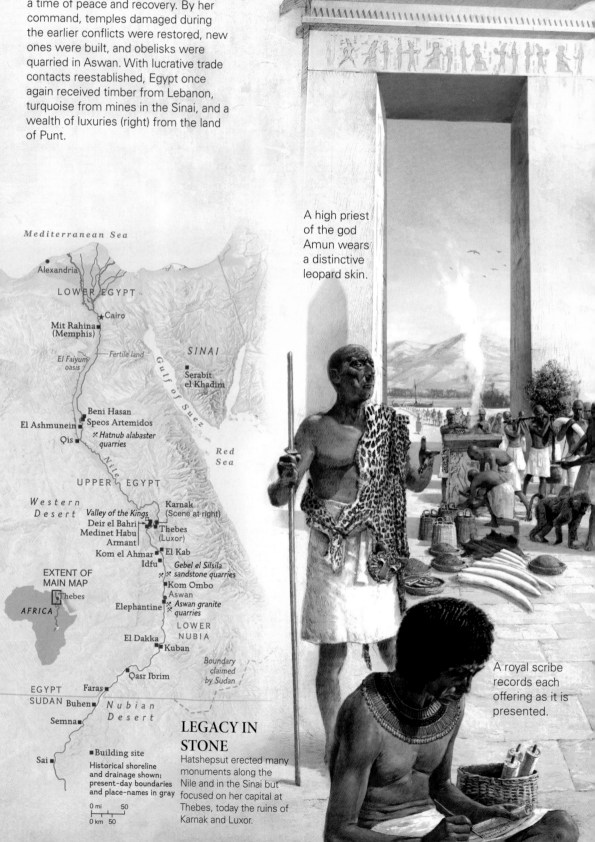

GLORIES OF HER REIGN

In the wake of the campaigns fought by her predecessors at the dawn of the New Kingdom, Hatshepsut ushered in a time of peace and recovery. By her command, temples damaged during the earlier conflicts were restored, new ones were built, and obelisks were quarried in Aswan. With lucrative trade contacts reestablished, Egypt once again received timber from Lebanon, turquoise from mines in the Sinai, and a wealth of luxuries (right) from the land of Punt.

A high priest of the god Amun wears a distinctive leopard skin.

A royal scribe records each offering as it is presented.

Map labels

Mediterranean Sea

Alexandria

LOWER EGYPT

★ Cairo

Mit Rahina (Memphis)

El Faiyum oasis — *Fertile land*

SINAI

■ Serabit el Khadim

Beni Hasan
Speos Artemidos
✕ *Hatnub alabaster quarries*

El Ashmunein

Qis

Gulf of Suez

Red Sea

Nile

UPPER EGYPT

Western Desert

Karnak (Scene at right)

Valley of the Kings
Deir el Bahri
Medinet Habu
Armant

Thebes (Luxor)

Kom el Ahmar

El Kab

Idfu

Gebel el Silsila ✕ sandstone quarries

✕ Kom Ombo

Aswan
✕ *Aswan granite quarries*

Elephantine

EXTENT OF MAIN MAP

☐ Thebes

AFRICA

LOWER NUBIA

El Dakka

■ Kuban

Boundary claimed by Sudan

EGYPT
SUDAN

Faras

Buhen

Nubian Desert

Semna

Sai

■ Building site

Historical shoreline and drainage shown; present-day boundaries and place-names in gray

0 mi   50
0 km   50

LEGACY IN STONE

Hatshepsut erected many monuments along the Nile and in the Sinai but focused on her capital at Thebes, today the ruins of Karnak and Luxor.

THE RICHES OF PUNT

Early in her rule as king, Hatshepsut sent trading ships to Punt, a land somewhere along Africa's Red Sea coast. When the ships returned, priests at Karnak presented a dazzling array of goods to the pharaoh, who dedicated it all to Amun, her patron god.

Thutmose III stands next to Hatshepsut, the proper place of a co-ruler on official occasions.

Hatshepsut wears the nemes headcloth with its sacred cobra.

The pharaoh waves a sekhem scepter over the offerings.

Pharaonic regalia includes a false beard.

Imports from Punt include circular gold ingots (right), spices, tusks, ebony, myrrh trees for incense, panther skins, and live baboons.

FERNANDO G. BAPTISTA AND AMANDA HOBBS, NG STAFF

SOURCE: W. RAYMOND JOHNSON, ORIENTAL INSTITUTE OF THE UNIVERSITY OF CHICAGO

MAP: CHARLES BERRY

(Continued from page 09) vengeance on his unscrupulous stepmother fell apart. A more logical scenario was devised around the possibility that Thutmose III needed to reinforce the legitimacy of his son Amenhotep II's succession in the face of rival claims from other family members. And Hatshepsut, once disparaged for ruthless ambition, is now admired for her political skill.

"Nobody can know what she was like," says Catharine Roehrig, now a curator in the same department once headed by Hayes. "She ruled for 20 years because she was capable of making things work. I believe she was very canny and that she knew how to play one person off against the next—without murdering them or getting murdered herself."

Last spring photographer Kenneth Garrett asked Wafaa El Saddik, director of the Egyptian Museum in Cairo, to review a list of Hatshepsut treasures he hoped to photograph for this article: a limestone sphinx of Hatshepsut from the ruins of her temple, the wooden box containing the tooth, a limestone bust of Hatshepsut in the guise of the underworld god Osiris. El Saddik came to the final item on the list: the mummified body of Hatshepsut herself. "You want us to remove the glass?" she asked incredulously, as if the mummy, long neglected, now possessed something

It was not long... before this vain, ambitious, and unscrupulous woman showed herself in her true colors.

unspeakably precious. The photographer nodded. The director shuddered. "This is the history of the world we're talking about!" she exclaimed.

In the end, it was decreed that one of the panels of glass could be removed from the case in the Royal Mummy Room without jeopardizing the history of the world. Staring at what was left of the great female pharaoh as the lights were being set up, I found myself wondering why it was so important to authenticate her corpse. On the one hand, what could better animate the astonishing history of ancient Egypt than the actual woman preserved in defiance of nature and the forces of decay? Here she was now, among us, like an ambassador of antiquity.

On the other hand, what did we want from her? Wasn't there something oppressively morbid about the curiosity that brought millions of rubberneckers to the Royal Mummy Rooms and made a fetish of the royal dead in the first place? The longer I stared at Hatshepsut, the more I recoiled from those unfathomable eyes and the suffocating fixity of that lifeless flesh. Most of us live by the lapwing creed that is the antithesis of the pharaohs' faith: ashes to ashes, dust to dust. It struck me how much more of Hatshepsut was alive in her texts, where even after so many thousands of years, you can still feel the flutter of her heart.

Discussion Questions:

- What investigative and scientific methods were used to discover Hatshepsut's mummy? Why do you think Brown spends so much time describing these methods?

- Why do you think Brown includes information on why Hatshepsut tried to preserve her legacy? How does that information relate to the other details he provides about her?

- Brown has two focal points in this article: how Hatshepsut's mummy was found and how she ruled. Do you think that the article should be split in two so that each part could be dealt with in more depth?

- Why do you think Brown included a section on how archeologists overturned historians' view of Hatshepsut as an "evil stepmother"? Was this relevant to his main focus? If so, how?

Writing Activities

- Percy Bysshe Shelley's poem "Ozymandias" focuses on the legacy of the Egyptian king Rameses (1304–1237 B.C.) One of Shelley's main themes in the poem is the transitory nature of power and influence. Write a brief analysis of the poem and determine whether or not it could apply to Hatshepsut's legacy and influence. Refer in your essay to the following words that she had written on her obelisk: "Now my heart turns this way and that, as I think what the people will say. Those who see my monuments in years to come, and who shall speak of what I have done."

- Compare and contrast the rule of a 20th-century female head of state with that of Hatshepsut. In your analysis, explore each ruler's rise to power and her successes and failures as a ruler. Discuss any impact you feel that their gender may have had on these successes and failures.

- Write an analysis of the ways that Hatshepsut had to accept and break traditions in order to gain and maintain her power.

Collaborative Activities

- Each member of your group will choose a 20th-century female ruler and research her rise to power along with her successes and failures. Your group will then determine the two most successful rulers and present the basis for your determination to the class.

- In groups, discuss the difficulties Hatshepsut faced ruling as a woman. How did Hatshepsut gain and maintain power, given the fact that she was a woman? What traditions did she accept? Which did she challenge? Do you think women today face the same difficulties when trying to rise to a position of power in American society? Prepare to present your position to the class.

- Discuss in your group the ways Hatshepsut tried to preserve her legacy. Why do you think this was so important to her?

CHOLITAS FIGHT BACK!

Alma Guillermoprieto reports on the popularity of
female wrestling in Bolivia in her article "Cholitas Fight
Back!" She includes interviews of "cholitas," the native
Aymara women dressed in traditional costumes who
battle each other in the ring.

**As you read "Cholitas Fight Back!" you should
consider the following questions:**

- Why do the women participate in this sport?
- Why is the sport so popular?
- What effect does the sport have on the wrestlers'
  lives?

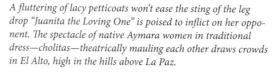

*A fluttering of lacy petticoats won't ease the sting of the leg
drop "Juanita the Loving One" is poised to inflict on her oppo-
nent. The spectacle of native Aymara women in traditional
dress—cholitas—theatrically mauling each other draws crowds
in El Alto, high in the hills above La Paz.*

CHOLITAS FIGHT BACK

Photographs by Ivan Kashinsky

Ardent fans strain to touch Juanita the Loving One as she bursts from behind the curtain and strides toward the ring. The fighting cholitas see themselves as symbols of strength: Their opponents include bigotry and sexism. "My goal," says one fighter, "is to lift up indigenous women, who have been treated with contempt."

THE PRETTILY DRESSED

CHOLITAS WALLOPING EACH OTHER

ELICIT AUDIENCE CHEERS. FOR AT LEAST A FEW HOURS, EVERYONE FORGETS THE TROUBLES OF REALITY.

At the largest public gymnasium in El Alto, Bolivia, daylight is fading from the windows, and hundreds of people along the bleachers are growing impatient. They have been sitting for more than two hours now, jeering and whistling and yelling encouragement at the succession of *artistas* who have faced off in the center of the gym to match wits and perform dazzling feats of strength and skill. But it is growing late, and over the blaring disco music, foot-stomping and impatient whistles can be heard in crescendo: "Bring them on!" The music grows louder, the whistling too; there is a sense that rebellion may be about to erupt, but at last the houselights flash and dim, and the music shifts to the *chunka-chunka* beat of a modern Bolivian *huayño*. An announcer emotes into the microphone, the curtains leading to the locker rooms part, and "Amorous Yolanda" and "Evil Claudina," this evening's stars, make their longed-for appearance to ecstatic applause.

Like many of the women of Aymara descent in the audience, Yolanda and Claudina are dressed to the nines in the traditional fashion of the Andean highlands: shiny skirts over layers of petticoats, embroidered shawls

Welcome to the delirious world of Bolivian wrestling.

pinned with filigreed jewelry, bowler hats. Their costumes glisten in the spotlights while they make a regal progress around the bleachers, greeting their public with the genteel smiles of princesses, twirling and waving gracefully until the music stops. That's the sign for the two women to swing themselves deftly onto the wrestling ring that has been the focus of this afternoon's activity. Swiftly they remove their hats, unpin their shawls, and...*whap, whap, whap!* Claudina belts Yolanda one, Yolanda slaps Claudina, Claudina tries to escape, but Yolanda grabs Claudina by her pigtails and spins her around, and *WHAM!* Claudina whirls through the air, petticoats and braids flying, and lands flat on her back on the mat, gasping like a fish. The audience goes nuts.

Welcome to the delirious world of Bolivian wrestling. In the cold, treeless, comfortless city of *(Continued on page 20)*

Adapted from "Bolivia's Women Wrestlers: Cholitas Fight Back" by Alma Guillermoprieto: National Geographic Magazine, September 2008.

Hundreds pack a gymnasium in El Alto each Sunday to see the Titans of the Ring clash. Ticket sales for the originally all-male lucha libre program—$1.50 for locals, and a few dollars more for curious foreigners (who get perks like front-row seats and a guide)—boomed after organizer Juan Mamani added women wrestlers to the lineup in 2001.

(Continued from page 17) El Alto ("high point"), 13,000 feet above sea level, there are one million people, most of whom fled here over the past three decades to escape the countryside's pervasive misery. The lucky ones find steady jobs down in the capital city of La Paz, which El Alto overlooks. Many sell clothes, onions, pirated DVDs, Barbie dolls, car parts, small desiccated mammals for magic rituals. The poorest *alteños* employ themselves as beasts of burden. All of them battle hopeless traffic, a constant scarcity of fuel and water, the dull fatigue of numbing labor, the odds that are stacked against them. When they're done working, they need to play, and when they want to play, one never knows what they will come up with. Lately, they've come up with the extraordinary spectacle of the *cholitas luchadoras*—fighting cholitas—which has given new life to Bolivians' own version of Mexican *lucha libre,* a free-form spectacle somewhere between a passion play, a wrestling match, and bedlam.

"Watch out!" the entire audience shrieks. Yolanda has been celebrating her victory, but Claudina, as proof of her evil nature, is about to lunge at her from behind. Yolanda spins too late; Claudina knocks her flat and clambers like a crazy person onto the ropes. "I'm the prettiest!" she yells at the audience. "You're all ugly! I'm your daddy! I'm the one the gringos have come to see!" Indeed three rows of ringside seats are filled with foreigners, all pop-eyed, but they're actually irrelevant. It's their fellow Bolivians the cholitas are performing for.

Claudina, who is officially a *ruda,* or baddie, has taken a swig of soda pop and is spraying the public with it at the precise moment that Yolanda, a *técnica,* or goodie, pounces on her and drags her up to the bleachers, sending the spectators there scattering in blissful, screaming alarm. Yolanda wins! No, Claudina wins! No, Yolanda! But wait! The audience screams in warning again because a new menace has silently made his entrance: "Black Abyss"—or maybe it's "Satanic Death" or the "White Skeleton"; it's hard to keep track—has leaped into the fray and has Yolanda in a ferocious leg lock. The situation looks hopeless, but no, here comes the "Last Dragon," out of nowhere, and he's carrying a chair! And he's whomping Black Abyss, or maybe the Skeleton, or maybe Yolanda, on the head with it! Even Claudina seems to have lost track of who's who: She's taking a flying leap at her own ally, the loathsome "Picudo." "He is destroyed forever!" the announcer yells frenetically.

Or almost forever: In lucha libre, no defeat is ever final.

"**W**hat I want to make absolutely clear," says Juan Mamani, who fights as a *rudo* under the lucha name of "El Gitano" and who runs the show, "is that it was me who came up with the idea of the cholitas." Mamani is a tall, angular man whom it would be kind to call unfriendly. He cuts phone conversations short by hanging up, does not show up for appointments he has been cornered into making, and tries to charge for interviews. His cholitas are terrified of him. "Don't tell him you called me; don't tell him you have my phone number!" one of them begged.

I hunted him down near the El Alto gym, and after an unpromising start—he kept trying to duck past me—I said the magic words "Mexico" and "Blue Demon." The face of Juan Mamani, the ogre, was suddenly wreathed in smiles. "My greatest passion is lucha libre," he said. "And for us, Mexico is the example. Blue Demon is for me *lo mas grandioso.*"

Mamani's wrestlers all hold daytime jobs, and he makes a living from a small electrical-repair shop. But he has invested a good part of his life's earnings in a huge wrestling ring at home, where his group trains. He pays his wrestlers between $20 and $30 a match and probably doesn't clear vastly greater amounts himself. "Here in Bolivia it's impossible to make a living from this great passion of mine," Mamani said. His dream was to create a Bolivian school of wrestling heroes to equal the feats of the great Mexican lucha legends; their daring leaps and backflips, their unique costumes and regal bearing. Had I seen Blue Demon fight? Really? He shook my hand as I left.

About seven years ago, when he was fretting about the diminishing audience for the weekly lucha libre spectacle at the El Alto gym, Mamani had the inspired idea to teach women to wrestle and put them in the ring in cholita clothes. "Martha la Alteña," an outgoing luchadora, not remarkably muscular but very strong, was among the 60 or so young women who answered Mamani's open audition call. Like several of the eight or so who ended up staying, she comes from a wrestling background. "My father was one of the original Mummies," she said proudly, referring to one of the best loved, or most dreaded, of Bolivian lucha's creatures.

Amorous Yolanda was also inspired by her *luchador* father, and even though her parents separated on unfriendly terms when she was an infant, she used to sneak into El Coliseo in downtown La Paz—long since gone—to watch him perform. "But a lot of times men don't believe in women," she told me. "Once I heard my father say that he wished he'd had a son instead of me, so he could follow in his footsteps as a luchador." When she heard about Mamani's casting call, Yolanda, then still called Veraluz Cortés, raced to audition, leading to a temporary rift with her father. Whether her lucha stardom also contributed to the breakup of her marriage is not clear.

Outside the ring, Martha la Alteña generally wears what is called the señorita style of dress—blue jeans and sweaters—and part of the glamour of her cholita costume is provided by turquoise-blue contact lenses. Yolanda, on the other hand, who is thin and

It's a distraction. The cholitas fight here, and we laugh and forget our troubles for three or four hours. At home, we're sad.

very intense, wears a bowler hat and petticoats and skirts, even when she is knitting sweaters at her day job, and considers herself an authentic cholita.

"Sometimes my daughters ask why I insist on doing this," she said. "It's dangerous; we have many injuries, and my daughters complain that wrestling does not bring any money into the household. But I need to improve every day. Not for myself, for Veraluz, but for the triumph of Yolanda, an artist who owes herself to her public."

Esperanza Cancina, 48, who sells used clothing for a living, has installed her large family and her ample self, in all her petticoats and skirts, in the choice ringside spot behind the announcer's chair, at a safe angle from the popcorn and chicken bones and empty plastic bottles the audience likes to pelt the rudos with. Ringside seats cost about $1.50 each, which is hardly cheap, but Señora Cancina comes faithfully to the show every other Sunday. "It's a distraction," she explains. "The cholitas fight here, and we laugh and forget our troubles for three or four hours. At home, we're sad."

Around us, the youngest members of the audience, including her grandchildren, are skittering around the edges of the ring in an adrenaline frenzy, trying out lucha leaps and swarming after a wrestler who has just been defeated, trying to hug him, touch his costume. The music is booming, and it's hard to conduct a conversation, but Señora Cancina is amiable and cooperative. She had 12 children, she says, but after a pause adds that six died. How? Her face takes on a distressing blankness. "Scarlet fever, diarrhea, those things…" she murmurs, and has to repeat the answer over the noise. Would she have wanted to be a luchadora (Continued on page 24)

Her slight form bulked up by the many layers of her pollera skirt, "Amorous Yolanda" humbles burly "Craquen." Female fans relish victories over male wrestlers by tough cholitas—scripted though they are. "I am a loving person outside the ring," Yolanda says. "But once in the ring, Amorous Yolanda becomes 'Hateful Yolanda.'"

(Continued from page 21) too? Definitely, she says. "Our husbands make fools of us, but if we were wrestlers we could express our fury."

Over on the long side of the bleachers, in the prime chicken-bone-throwing area, Rubén Copa, a shoemaker from La Paz with an easy, friendly smile, is waiting impatiently for the afternoon's final match—one in which the "Mummy Ramses II" will take on cholitas yet to be announced. "Bolivian wrestlers aren't half bad, you know," he says with a touch of pride. Not even the women? He huffs and waves his hands in protest. "There's none of that anymore! Every kind of work is for everyone now." I want to know if it's true that men come to the lucha libre just to see the cholitas' (very modest) underpants. For a moment he looks offended, but then he smiles again. "Not at all!" he says. "I come to see them wrestle! You'll see for yourself how good they are."

And indeed a few minutes later the Mummy Ramses II is staggering around invincibly in a red-stained jumpsuit and a fright wig, dragging one cholita behind him while another one looks for something to set him on fire with, and the kids are screaming in delicious terror, and Señora Cancina is yelling things at the Mummy that cannot be printed in this magazine, grinning broadly as she does so. The Mummy is slamming his victim against the wall, and it looks tough for the cholitas, as the announcer warns us, in this *definitivo y final combate*—it looks very, very tough. But something tells me that you can't keep a cholita down.

Here comes Martha, flying through the air!

Discussion Questions

- What is Guillermoprieto's tone in the article? How do you think she views the women? The sport?

- Why do you think Guillermoprieto chose the title? What do you think the women are "fighting back" against?

- What is the author's attitude toward Juan Mamani, who runs the wrestling shows? Why do you think the author included information about him in the article?

- Why do you think the author avoids talking about whether or not the women can get seriously hurt in the ring?

Writing Activities

- Research the popularity of female professional wrestling in the United States. Write an essay comparing and contrasting the sport in the U.S. and in Bolivia, exploring differences in its popularity and in what motivates women to enter the ring. Determine whether or not cultural issues can account for these differences.

- Watch the 2008 film *The Wrestler* and write an essay that analyzes the main character's experience in and outside of the ring. How do his experiences compare with those of the women in "Cholitas Fight Back!"? How do gender roles influence these experiences?

- One of the main reasons women participate in this sport is to earn money. Write an essay that investigates what, if anything, the Bolivian government is trying to do to alleviate the high poverty rate in that country.

Collaborative Activities

- Form groups to examine the popularity of this controversial sport. Interview supporters as well as critics of professional wrestling, and present your findings to the class.

- Discuss what jobs in the United States poor women are forced to take in order to support their families. Choose two of these jobs and research the effects they have on the women who must accept them. Present your findings to the class.

HIMBA: CONSULTING THE PAST, DIVINING THE FUTURE

In "Himba: Consulting the Past, Divining the Future," Karen E. Lange writes of how the Himba tribe in Nambia preserves solid links to the past while confronting changes that threaten its survival. Lange focuses primarily on the women in the tribe and the rituals they perform in order to maintain a strong sense of community.

As you read "Himba: Consulting the Past, Divining the Future," you should consider the following questions:

- What changes have threatened the survival of the tribe?
- How have tradition and adaptation helped the tribe survive?
- What powerful role do women play in the tribe?

Bodies glowing with butterfat and red with ocher, Himba women in northwestern Namibia are sought by tourists looking for "traditional" Africa. But Himba ways are changing fast as these herders negotiate their place in a young nation, independent since 1990. While most of the women still wear skins, they are beginning to vote, send their children to school, and count wealth in cash as well as in cattle. Women hold on to Himba dress in part because the larger world of jobs and politics remains closed to them, says anthropologist Margaret Jacobsohn. Their husbands and sons, who have more chances to earn wages in towns, are likely to mix Western clothes with traditional garb.

HIMBA:
CONSULTING
THE PAST
DIVINING THE
FUTURE

MOTHER TO DAUGHTER
Despite the increasing influence of the cash economy, Himba mothers remain highly honored for their life-giving power. "Money does not give birth," the Himba say. Girls become full adults only when they have children. At marriage a woman leaves her father's homestead to live with her husband's family, but she briefly returns to her mother to have her first baby. Rope wigs worn by girls about to start menstruating and ceremonial slings used by mothers to carry infants on special occasions are passed down from generation to generation within a line of women, signs of the potency of the matrilineage.

MIND, BODY, AND SOUL,

THE POWER OF HEALING

PROVES TO CONTRIBUTE TO THE SURVIVAL
OF THE HIMBA CULTURE.

When drought and war struck Namibia in the 1980s, it looked as if the culture of the indigenous Himba people might disintegrate. Ninety percent of Himba cattle, the center of their economy and identity, died. Some families left for Angola. Lacking any other means of survival and desperate for cash, a number of men joined South Africa's army in its fight against guerrillas seeking Namibian independence. Unable to feed themselves, Himba flowed into the town of Opuwo for relief food, settling in slums of cardboard and plastic sacks.

But the estimated 20,000 to 50,000 Himba, long among Africa's most prosperous herders, are resilient. In the 19th century those in Namibia survived cattle raids by marauding ethnic groups from the south. Most fled into Angola, joining with the Portuguese military and forming their own armies of raiders. Eventually many returned to Namibia. Starting in the 1920s, South African rulers confined them to a prescribed "homeland," officially forbidding them to trade, graze livestock freely, or garden and gather wild plants along the Kunene River. Yet they endured—even if at times it meant eating the hides they slept on.

Yet they endured—even if at times it meant eating the hides they slept on.

With the peace and good rains that came to Namibia in the 1990s, the Himba rebuilt their herds and, working with international activists, helped block a proposed hydro-electric dam that would have flooded ancestral lands along the Kunene. They also have benefited from new opportunities provided by the government of independent Namibia—mobile schools where Himba children learn English, and conservancies that give Himba control of wildlife and tourism on their lands. Vengapi Tijvinda, a grandmother in her 50s, lived through this rebirth. In the 1980s she was making baskets for tourists near Purros. Now she has returned to farming and raising goats and cattle: "Life is still the same, but the children can read and write. I am a member of [a] conservancy, and we have tasted game meat again."

Himba women believe that spirits of dangerous animals or the dead can enter their bodies and afflict them with physical illnesses—leading them to call on female healers, who perform

Adapted from "Himba: Consulting the Past, Divining the Future" by Karen E. Lange: National Geographic Magazine, January 2004.

exorcisms helped by other women. During the ritual, many of the woman fall into a trance. Anthropologist Jacobsohn sees such group trancing as a means for women to deal with unprecedented change—an influx of tourists, alcohol, children going to school, men working in towns for wages—that has robbed them of authority and left them uncertain about their role in society. "It's a way of handling conflict and stress. And conflict and stress have increased in the past 20 years."

A group trance may start as a party around a fire, with drinking, dancing, and plenty of meat, then shift to a healing, where women struggle with supernatural forces. Usually the otherworldly bellow of a special drum reserved for trancing calls every woman within hearing. They sit around the fire, swaying to the beat. "They go on and on and on," says Jacobsohn, who has witnessed such sessions. "Like teenagers at a rave." Slowly the women fall into trances. Some may suddenly exhibit possession. "I have seen people become three times as strong." Men looking on are deferential. If the women order them to do something, they quietly comply. For a night, at least, the women assert their power in the face of a future they cannot see and a present that challenges the past.

Discussion Questions

- Why do you think Lange included "Consulting the Past" in the title of this article?

- One of Lange's main points is that the Himba men and women are "resilient." How well does she prove this point? What examples does she use?

- Identify and analyze the way the author uses cause and effect as a rhetorical strategy. How effective is this method?

- How well do you think Lange explored the second part of her subtitle, "Divining the Future"? Are there any questions that you have that she did not answer regarding how the members of the tribe are facing the changes that are occurring around them?

Writing Activities

- Write an analytical essay on how the Himba survive by "consulting the past" as well as adapting to the present.

- Discuss in a personal essay how the women in your family have passed down traditions from generation to generation. What effect has the carrying on of tradition had in your family?

- Native Americans, like the Himba, have spiritual ties to nature. Research Native American spirituality and in an analytical essay, compare and contrast it with that of the Himba.

Collaborative Activities

- The article describes rituals that the Himba perform when girls reach adulthood. Discuss with your group what rituals Western cultures perform when their boys and girls become adults. Why do you think these rituals are important?

- Discuss the reasons the Himba fear changes to their homeland. What changes have you seen over the past decade in your community? Do any of them make you fearful or apprehensive?

ANATOMY OF A
BURMESE BEAUTY SECRET

In "Anatomy of a Burmese Beauty Secret," John M. Keshishian investigates a tribal custom practiced by the Padaung tribeswomen in Burma. When a girl is five, coils are wound around her neck, eventually pushing down her collarbones and ribs to the point that her neck appears to have grown longer, up to a foot. Keshishian explains that "the practice of wearing them helps maintain individual and tribal identity."

As you read "Anatomy of a Burmese Beauty Secret," you should consider the following questions:

- How is the tradition carried out?
- Why do the women in the tribe embrace this tradition?
- What damage does it do to the body?

ANATOMY OF A BURMESE BEAUTY SECRET

BEAUTY IS
IN THE EYES
OF THE BRASS HOLDER.

The land of the giraffe women.

A relentless embrace of brass, the burden of beauty shouldered by a Padaung tribeswoman of Burma armors the neck in a coil that weighs about 20 pounds, and measures a head-popping one foot high. The loops, draped with silver chains and coins and cushioned by a small pillow under the chin, signal elegance, wealth, and position.

But what is the anatomy beneath it all? Do the vertebrae stretch? Or do the ligaments binding them lengthen? Perhaps the disk spaces expand? An invitation to lecture at Burma's three medical schools enabled me to unravel the secret of the long-necked women.

At the Rangoon General Hospital I tracked down the X rays of a Padaung woman admitted for diagnostic tests. As fans swished lazily overhead, the films on view boxes illuminated the mystery. The neck hadn't been stretched at all. In effect, the chest had been pushed down. Each added loop increased pressure downward on the vertebral column. Something had to give—and did. The clavicles, or collarbones, as well as the ribs, had been gradually pushed down. The result of this displacement: a neck that just looks elongated.

"The land of the giraffe women," as Polish explorer Vitold de Golish called it, lies in eastern Burma on a high plateau dimpled by terraced, paddy-filled valleys. Here live the Padaung, a tribe of about 7,000 members.

Legend claims that the brass rings protect the women from tiger bites, but actually the practice of wearing them helps maintain individual and tribal identity.

A brass rod a third of an inch in diameter is worked around a girl's neck at about 5 years of age by a village medicine man. After divination with chicken bones to determine the most auspicious date, several loops are twisted around her neck. Additional loops are added periodically.

Rings worn on arms and legs may weigh a woman down with an *(Continued on page 38)*

Adapted from "Anatomy of a Burmese Beauty Secret" by John M. Keshishian, M.D.: National Geographic Magazine, June 1979.

(Continued from page 35) additional thirty pounds of brass. Since leg coils hamper walking, the women waddle. Constrained from drinking in the usual head-back position, a ring wearer leans forward to sip through a straw. And the voices of wearers, wrote British journalist J. G. Scott, sound "as if they were speaking up the shaft of a well."

After years of being straitjacketed in brass, the neck muscles atrophy. If the rings are cut off, a brace must support the neck until exercises rebuild the muscles.

In past times the punishment for adultery decreed removal of the coils. The head then flopped over, and suffocation could follow.

Two decades ago the encroachment of modern civilization prompted some women to remove their rings, though years of wearing them had left striations. The custom, indelibly inscribed in Padaung culture, persists and, according to University of Illinois anthropologist F. K. Lehman, shows signs of a resurgence.

Discussion Questions

- What is the author's tone in the article? How do his words help reveal his attitude toward this tradition?

- How is the title of the article ironic?

- An explorer called the area where the Padaung tribe resides, the "land of the giraffe women." What connotations does this phrase evoke?

- Why is it appropriate that the author is a medical doctor? How would the article be written differently from the point of view of an anthropologist or historian?

Writing Activities

- Analyze in an essay how society puts pressure on women to conform to its definition of beauty.

- Interview women and men who have adorned their bodies with tattoos and or piercings. Write about what causes these men and women to decorate themselves in this way and what effect tattoos and piercings have on their sense of themselves.

Collaborative Activities

- Discuss ways that contemporary women mutilate their bodies in order to be considered more attractive. Do you think they do this for the same reasons the Burmese women wear the coils?

- Discuss in your group whether self-mutilation should be banned. Take a position either for or against and be ready to debate this topic with the rest of the class.

- Investigate how women in other countries have been mutilated in the name of beauty or status.

THE TURKISH REPUBLIC COMES OF AGE

In "The Turkish Republic Comes of Age," Maynard Owen Williams writes about how women in Turkey at the close of World War II had gained new rights and opportunities previously given only to men. Williams also notes, however, that inequality for women still existed in Turkey during that period.

As you read "The Turkish Republic Comes of Age," you should consider the following questions:

- What new freedoms had Turkish women gained by 1945?
- In what ways were they still restricted?
- What encouraged Turkish women to hope for more freedom in the future?

Faces and Arms Are Bare, but Minds Are Clothed in Knowledge
Their obvious vigor contrasts with the idleness of harem beauties who, sheltered from books and society, lived in ignorance. Were such a one to appear on the streets in veil today, small boys would hoot.

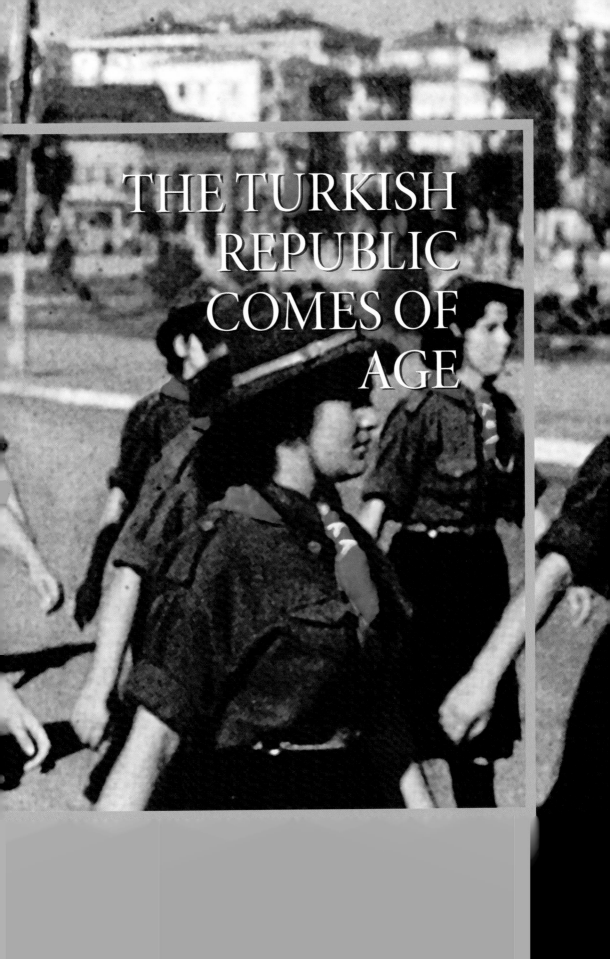

THE TURKISH REPUBLIC COMES OF AGE

GOULD HALL

THE AMERICAN COLLEGE FOR G

Better than Words in Stone, Bobby Socks Prove American College for Girls Is American
In the twenties bobbed hair and middy blouses were the rage. Overlooking the Bosporus at Arnautköy, the school is a neighbor of Robert College (for boys). Originally a high school, American College confers degrees on Turkish, Greek, American, and other girls. Graduates have had wide influence in emancipating Moslem women.

TURKEY LEAPED IN ONE GENERATION AFTER WORLD WAR I FROM A RIGIDLY PATRIARCHAL SOCIETY TO

A MORE OPEN ONE FOR WOMEN.

A WRITER IN THE 1940s EXPECTED EVEN MORE FOR THEIR FUTURE.

The Turkish Republic is now of age.

On the day Turkey, by unanimous vote of the Grand National Assembly, broke off diplomatic relations with Germany, I watched the ferryboats leave Istanbul's Galata Bridge and disperse, lest vengeful bombs disrupt the traffic of the city by the Golden Horn.

August 4, 1944, at Ankara's big, clean station, I saw Franz von Papen make an inglorious exit while a few misguided Axis puppets gave the Nazi salute and waved handbags and hats in front of the press cameras.

Hundreds of poker-faced Turks silently watched a shiny private car, attached to the crack Anadolu Express, bear the German Ambassador away. Five minutes later the broad platform was empty, the restaurant loudspeaker was at full blast, and thick Turkish coffee was being inhaled with noisy gusto.

In 1911, when I first went to Turkey, it was a huge Empire which stretched from Balkan snows to Libian sands. But World War I stripped it of vast territory, including Palestine, Syria, and Arabia.

Turkey's strong man, successively known as Mustafa Kemal Pasha, the Ghazi, and Kemal Atatürk, divorced the Moslem Church (Islam) and the State from a union which had endured for 1,200 years. He moved the capital from Constantinople (Istanbul) to Ankara and on October 29, 1923, proclaimed the Turkish Republic.

The fez was abolished, and elder men in caps turned the visors back, like old-time aviators and movie directors, so that their reverent foreheads could touch the footstool of Allah the Merciful.

Setting up his blackboard in the very shadow of the once-sweet-scented seraglio, Kemal Atatürk taught his people a new alphabet, akin to our own. Even he dared not rudely tear aside the veil. But when the new railway to Kayseri was opened, only unveiled women got the choice seats!

To help them carry out his dictum, "Be Proud," he sought to imbue Turks with a knowledge of their history, which goes back to the days when men were first cultivating grain and domesticating animals.

Adapted from "The Turkish Republic Comes of Age" by Maynard Owen Williams: National Geographic Magazine, May 1945.

The memory of Atatürk, reinforced by many a monument and countless pictures, lives on. His hardly, homogeneous people, led by President İsmet İnönü, are working out their own destiny. The Turkish Republic is now of age.

From the car window during the hot ride last summer from Kayseri to Ankara, it would have been easy to believe that no progress had been made. Peasants in many-patched clothing were treading out the grain in the immemorial way. Peasant women, dressed in Turkey-red pantaloons and with their head shawls pulled close about their faces, looked unchanged.

But never had I seen such fine flocks and herds along these valleys where young trees were spreading their shade. Wheat was piled high. And at Ankara it was as if some Aladdin had rubbed his magic lamp.

When, in 1927, I toured the new republic with truck, tent, and interpreter, I had seen some of the first new buildings of Ankara rise from the forbidding plain. Malarial mosquitoes reigned in the low swampland, and the passing of every vehicle was marked by a cloud of dust.

Today, white-sailed "yachts" tack back and forth on the pleasure lake which has replaced the miasmic swamps, and Diesel-motored buses roll down such boulevards as few cities know.

Countless trees shade the broad highways. In every quarter there are parks and flower beds galore. At sidewalk cafes young men in fashionable dress eat their cakes and ices in cosmopolitan ease. Their fathers wrestled with the serpentlike tubes of gurgling narghiles.

New Freedoms of Turkish Women

Were Turkey still the man's world it was, with women decked like black crows within "yes" distances of their lords, Ankara would be a remarkable city. Through it now move pretty young Turkish girls, short of skirt, sheer of stocking, and red of lip, with freedom and poise. Cork-platformed sandals add to their streamlined height.

Male influence still exerts its conservatism on them. There are many things that these slim princesses may not do. But so far as I could judge, they are as independent as American girls. These free-striding young women seem the finest fruits of the New Turkey.

From the Turkish Press and Printing Bureau, where I got my press card, Nuri Eren and I drove to a modern broadcasting studio. A recording was being made for transmission to America. Few studios have finer equipment.

Perhaps it was the glow of the young woman announcer, who was wearing a new engagement ring; but every time this dark-eyed girl spoke over the microphone it was as if an inarticulate race of women suddenly had found voice.

Here is a quotation from her broadcast:
Listen, America!
We are the women of Turkey!
We are free, as our country is free.
We have won our liberty and we cherish it.
Like you, we have equal rights with men.
Listen, America!
We are the women of Turkey!

Within sight of Ankara is Atatürk's farm, now operated by the State. Where pure milk and butter are prepared for market, blooded stock is raised, and modern farming methods are taught, I found five stalwart young men gravely listening to one small woman.

In what began as a modest repair shop, new spare parts for Case and McCormick threshing machines and tractors were being forged, and thousands of plows were being turned out with assembly-line dispatch.

Another excursion from Ankara was to Hasanoğlan, once visited for its crude carvings from a remote past. But today Hasanoğlan is a typical experiment station for the Turkish peasant.

The first party of young men arriving at the site brought their own food and slept in tents. Today their huge dining hall has a sloping floor and doubles as a theater. Fifty-one excellent buildings are already completed and more are in construction. All this has been done by the boys and girls themselves, with a minimum of supervision.

Village Institutes Aid Farmers

Of the 760 students at this one Village Institute, 100 are girls who weave fabrics, study to be midwives, sew, study music, painting, and dancing while the young men are tilling the fields, threshing the crops, or adding new units to the ground plan.

Turkey's peasants constitute 80 percent of the country's population. They live in more than 40,000 widely scattered villages, few of which have any schools. Much as teachers are needed, a mere teacher would be a luxury in a poverty-stricken hamlet. Certainly a city-trained teacher would not be happy there.

Until the peasants develop more earning power—and wartime prices which now favor them cannot last forever—it has seemed desirable to train young peasants who can teach rudimentary subjects and also add to the current earning power of the village. Heavier sheaves, bigger udders, sturdier stock—those are lessons the peasants understand.

By means of the Village Institutes, boys and girls born to the Village environment and trained in the open countryside are sent back to help solve Turkey's basic problem—a poverty-stricken and unschooled rural population.

In 1935–36, when the huge new Government Center at Ankara had been completed at heavy expense, 6,901 teachers taught 370,000 villagers in a land of some 17,000,000 inhabitants. In 1942–43, 14,284 teachers taught 603,000 pupils.

6 out of 18 Village Institutes are already self-supporting, and thousands of graduates a year

But so far as I could judge, they are as independent as American girls. These free-striding young women seem the finest fruits of the New Turkey.

are going out to lift the standard of Turkish village life.

In a school where masonry, gardening, well digging, husbandry, and weaving are required, one might expect purely academic subjects to be neglected. But in a 260-week course the equivalent of 114 weeks is devoted to cultural subjects, 58 to agricultural practice, 58 to technical work and shop, and 30 weeks to vacation.

During the current shortage of manpower in field and factory, many a Village Institute lad earns good money during his vacation.

As we arrived at Hasanoğlan, scores of young students were studying penmanship; others were raising timbers for a new roof. I inspected dozens of practice sheets. Turkey's villagers are better penmen than any class of high school or college students I knew at home.

Teaching Farmers to Farm

When an Institute student is graduated, he receives a plot of ground, some draft animals, and implements for improved farming. Classmates go with him and, beside the almost windowless homes of an adobe village, build him a new house with big windows and a door that will swing and latch. Then a school is built, and he becomes teacher, agricultural adviser, veterinary, and model citizen.

Before I left, after a double-size lunch with the Institute leaders, the director asked if I had any suggestions to make.

"Light is one of the chief needs in village homes," I replied. "Why don't you turn out some standard-sized window frames so that the villagers of Hasanoğlan can tear out a few mud bricks and let the daylight in?"

Before I finished, the director was chuckling.

"Fine idea!" he said. "That's just what we have been doing."

The old village is less than a mile from the neatly laid out Institute. But Hikmet Geray, a Robert College graduate, told how heavy is the weight of rural inertia.

"How many Institute students do you suppose we have been able to get from that village? The people go back and forth, see our crops and gardens, our airy dormitories, and neat girl students, our open-air theater, and our bright flower beds. How many of them have joined the procession toward a better life? Just two.

"Time and again we have tried to move villagers from played-out areas. Although there is coal near Zonguldak, our fields lack the fertility that they might have if we did not burn manure as fuel.

"The farmers, even when their crops are poor, resist change. They cling with superstitious caution to the fields they know.

"They say, 'These fields have been proved; the new ones haven't.' Yet all that some of their fields have proved is that the man who sticks to them will die poor.

"Soil analysis won't convince them. In a democracy you can't force them to abandon their old homes. But the Institute graduates wake them up, for on their new fields, scientifically chosen, they produce better crops. One thing a farmer can't stand is seeing his neighbor get a better yield than he does."

Women Forsake Rugmaking for Factories

At Sivas we visited a rug factory where little girls, following patterns which they must have learned in their cradles, were turning out choice carpets whose local price has advanced to about $4 a square foot.

Two unfinished rugs, still on the loom, had as their pattern a map of Turkey.

Lack of transportation, a change of dyes, the loss of Anatolian Greek carpet weavers—all have lessened the production of Turkish carpets. But a bigger factor is the high wages women can earn for other work. When there is a demand for women workers in modern factories, the tying of hundreds of intricate knots to a square inch becomes unduly expensive or inadequately paid.

If you have a rug dating back to the days when woman's place was the home, even though it was a felt tent in the heart of Turkistan, take good care of it. One produced today, and equally fine, will cost much more.

Across the road from the rug factory is a technical school whose products have professional quality. Hundreds of heavy vises were ready for shipment to less fortunate schools, and scores of cabinets, splendidly dovetailed and doweled, were being provided for sewing machines destined for remote villages. One machine may help fashion the dresses for a whole community.

In no other school have I seen larger or finer lathes. Sivas is coming to understand giant lathes very well, for it has a shop for building and repairing railway coaches and cars.

Near Sivas a new factory is turning out 300 tons of cement a day. Since New Turkey is defaced by many a crack in its stucco, I asked if the Sivas cement is really good.

"Our cement is pretty good," I was told. "But builders won't wash the sand and gravel. And the best cement isn't good if the sand and gravel are mixed with mud or dust."

Hastily he drew a diagram of the plant, showing how rock is brought in from the hills by overhead trolley and powdered coal is shipped in to the other end of the grounds.

"Out of season we can get all the labor we want at 20 piasters (15 cents) an hour," the director continued. "In plowing and threshing season, I have to pay twice as much; so I do all I can when labor is cheap. Luckily, our coal comes by rail and avoids Black Sea storms.

Fair and Sturdy, Country Women Smile for Geographic Readers Only because Their Menfolk Gave Permission
City styles and women's rights penetrate the interior slowly. However, these Cappadocia girls' mothers never languished in harems, but worked, faces seldom veiled, in the fields. Yet here several conceal the chin. Center: old style's black, baggy coverall, designed to hide the female form. Left: a two-piece adaptation.

"Up on the hillside we are building a big swimming pool and a reservoir. If my workers won't swim, they can at least have all the water they need for bathing."

Vivid Hours on a Turkish Train

I preferred to take the train back to Istanbul, close to the people, the green valley bottoms, the bright flocks, the singing wheels of the slow-paced oxcarts, the long piles of iron ore, the eternal merry-go-round of peasant threshing, the railside warehouses bursting with grain, and the bright flash of Turkoman costumes. Beneath the clear skies and tawny hills of the great plateau was the Rivieralike beauty of the Marmara shore and the ferry crossing, marked by the minarets of the Blue Mosque and Aya Sofia.

The Turks have opened vast vistas in Istanbul and built a sports stadium on the site of the vegetable gardens of Dolma Bahçe Palace. The Bosporus remains one of the most beautiful and majestic of waterways.

It took Robert College forty years—1863 to 1903—to produce its first Turkish graduate, Hüseyin Pektaş. His lovely daughters and our own children attended the same classes and swam together in the swift Bosporus.

His talented wife has been a member of the Grand National Assembly for years. Her combined broadcast to England with Miss Irene Ward of the British Parliament was a red-letter day for Turkish women.

When Gilbert Grosvenor, President of the National Geographic Society, was born on a beautiful hillside whence one looks across from Europe into Asia, the grandfather of Hüseyin Pektaş was sheik of the Pektaşi dervishes. Their cypress-candled *tekke* (monastery) crowned the hilltop above the Grosvenor home (Plate XVII).

The dervish sheik defied Sultan Abdul Hamid's order forbidding Turkish students to attend Robert College, and his grandson, who served as Ismet Inönü's secretary at the Lausanne Conference, is now the Vice President of Robert College.

Seated in their delightful home, I asked him and his alert wife whether Turkey still needs American aid in education.

"I can't foresee the time when we won't" was the prompt reply. "The irrefutable argument in favor of any type of education is the men it produces. Robert College and other American schools have produced the type of men Turkey needs."

"And the kind of women," added Madame Pektaş, both of whose attractive daughters are now on the staff of the American College for Girls.

Discussion Questions

- Williams describes the changes that occurred in Turkish society at the end of the war along with those involving women's roles. How had women's roles changed in Turkey? How much importance do you think he gave to these changes?

- What point was Williams making when he describes Turkish women in the past "decked like black crows within 'yes' distances of their lords"?

- What passages suggest that Williams supported new rights for women in Turkey?

- Consider the language Williams used to describe Turkish women. What words did he use that could be considered sexist?

Writing Activities

- Write an argumentative essay in which you state and defend your position on women wearing veils in public. In your essay, note any bans that currently exist.

- The graphic novel *Persepolis* and the film version of the book focus on the coming of age of an Iranian girl, who experiences some of the same type of restrictions as those imposed on Turkish girls. After reading the novel and/or watching the film, write an analysis of how the main character responds to these pressures.

Collaborative Activities

- Williams explained that some Turkish women in 1944 were no longer covering their faces. In the 21st century, a debate rages about whether veils should be banned in public. In your group, decide whether or not you support or reject this ban. Be prepared to present your position to the class.

- Research the status of women in Turkey in the 21st century. Have they gained equality? If not, what are they doing to try to gain equal rights?

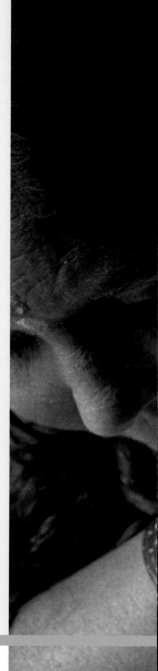

NECESSARY ANGELS

Tina Rosenberg reports in "Necessary Angels" on how women are being trained as village health workers in India. These women deliver babies, tend to the sick, and provide preventative care for 300 villages—half a million people in all.

As you read "Necessary Angels," you should consider the following questions:

- How did the health workers help the villagers?
- How are they trained?
- What are the long-term effects of their work?

Her fingers gnarled by leprosy suffered as a teenager. Sakubai Gite examines a two-year-old girl she delivered and still cares for.

NECESSARY
ANGELS

Photographs by Lynn Johnson

Founded in 1970, the CRHP (also known as Jamkhed, for the city where it is based) delivers preventive care to poor people who otherwise would get none. The project has served 300 villages and 500,000 people in Maharashtra state, including a newborn baby, fully swaddled and suspended for his weigh-in by village health worker Leelabai Amte.

THEY ARE NOT DOCTORS. THEY ARE NOT NURSES.
THEY ARE ILLITERATE WOMEN FROM INDIA'S UNTOUCHABLE CASTES.
YET AS TRAINED VILLAGE HEALTH WORKERS, THEY ARE DELIVERING BABIES, CURING DISEASE, AND SAVING LIVES—INCLUDING THEIR OWN.

Jawalke is a very different place because of Salve and Sathe.

When Sarubai Salve walks through her village, she gathers a crowd. Salve is 56, a slim, reserved, somewhat stern woman with wire-rimmed aviator glasses and long black hair streaked with gray. On most days she sets off twice, at nine in the morning and six at night, through the streets of Jawalke, a village of about 240 families in the central part of India's Maharashtra state. She carries a blood-pressure cuff, a stethoscope, a baby scale, and a thin logbook. She is often accompanied by Babai Sathe, an exuberant woman of 47, a bit zaftig, with a toothy smile.

The two of them are responsible for keeping Jawalke healthy. They deliver babies and then visit them. They see pregnant women and old people. They take blood pressure and check on villagers cured of leprosy.

Today, a sunny morning in January, the first patient they see is Rani Kale. The house where Kale is staying is made of mud, dirt, and cow dung with a thatched roof. A cat perches on one slope. In the yard, bricks are stacked up, clothes are slung over a line, and small fire pits hold twigs for cooking sorghum flatbread. A brown cow lies contentedly in the shade.

Kale is pregnant. If she were a resident of Jawalke, she would have been seen by Salve many times and sent to the hospital for a sonogram. But she is from a village an hour away. She has come to her mother's house to give birth.

This will be Kale's second baby. She has had no prenatal care until ten days ago, when she first arrived in Jawalke. Salve examined her and advised her to get a sonogram. But Kale never did, and now birth is days, or perhaps hours, away. Salve checks Kale's blood pressure, examines her nails and eyes for signs of anemia, and feels her legs for water retention. She takes Kale inside the hut and lays her on a mat for a pelvic exam. She puts her head on Kale's belly, listening to the heartbeat.

But Kale's belly is so tight that it is hard to detect anything. Sathe looks worried; she believes the baby is out of position. "But sometimes they move," she says. She tells

Adapted from "Necessary Angels" by Tina Rosenberg: National Geographic Magazine, December 2008.

Kale, "We'll come back in an hour or two. If the position is still not normal, we'll take you to the hospital. If you begin labor, just send someone for us." Salve asks one of Kale's aunts to give her tea. "Everything will be fine," she says reassuringly.

Next stop is the home of Manisha Mane, mother of a three-month-old boy with a cleft palate. Sathe and Salve watch the baby suckle, and then put him in a sling and weigh him: nine pounds. Not enough. "You have to supplement," says Salve. They tell Mane how to make a porridge of sorghum, oil, and vegetables. They show her where the baby falls on a growth chart and talk about vaccinations. After tending to Mane's mother-in-law, who suffers from hypertension, Sathe stops at a kindergarten where a government worker is scheduled to give vaccines. When word gets out, the kindergarten quickly becomes a makeshift clinic. Pregnant women and mothers of newborns stop in, and older women come in for blood-pressure checks.

Jawalke is a very different place because of Salve and Sathe. Salve has been doing rounds in Jawalke since 1984. By her own count, she has delivered 551 babies and says she's never lost a single infant or mother. "When I started, the children all had scabies and there was filth everywhere," she says. Small kids used to die. Pregnant women died during and after delivery. Poor sanitation led to malaria and diarrheal diseases. Children went unvaccinated. Leprosy and tuberculosis were common.

I ask Salve about Jawalke's health problems today. "Hypertension and diabetes," she says—rich-country illnesses. In most of rural India, only the fortunate suffer from such diseases.

The shortage of doctors in poor countries is widely lamented, especially in English-speaking countries such as Ghana, Malawi, and India, where doctors often leave for high-paying jobs abroad. They are pushed to leave by abysmal conditions—major hospitals may have only a handful of doctors and a dozen nurses to care for hundreds. Patients die unnecessarily. Pay is terrible and often months late. But doctors and nurses are also pulled to places like the United States, Canada, Britain, and Australia. These countries don't have doctors willing to work in rural areas or enough nurses at all. They fill the gap with health professionals from poor countries.

The result is that Africa and to a lesser extent India now effectively subsidize medicine in the U.S. and Britain. Ghana, Malawi, and Zimbabwe are among 16 African nations with more doctors practicing outside their countries than in them. In recent years the number of nurses leaving Malawi for jobs has outstripped the number graduating from nursing school. The medical brain drain is a problem being discussed by the G8 forum of the world's richest countries, the WHO, and Harvard University, among others.

But enticing doctors and nurses to stay home may not be the answer to the health care crisis in poor countries. I asked Nils Daulaire, the head of a U.S. based group called the Global Health Council, what can be done about the fact that there are only, for example, roughly three doctors for every 150,000 people in Malawi.

"Can we get it down to two? Or one?" he said.

Daulaire was only half joking. Doctors, he says, are not the solution for the world's poorest people. Even if they do not emigrate, doctors stay in the cities. In Malawi half of the country's doctors work in just one of four hospitals in major cities, although Malawi is about 85 percent rural. With a handful of exceptions, doctors in poor countries become doctors for the same reason most people all over the world do: to make a good living. If Malawi or India does succeed in recruiting a doctor for a health post in the countryside, chances are that a patient looking for him there will not find him. He will be in the capital, treating patients who can pay.

Even doctors who do treat villagers, moreover, rarely spend time teaching them about nutrition, breast-feeding, hygiene, and using home remedies such as oral rehydration solutions. They don't help villages acquire clean water and sanitation systems or improve their farming practices—ways to eliminate the root causes of disease. They don't work to dispel myths that keep people sick. They don't combat the discrimination against women and low-caste people that is toxic to good health. Doctors also present a powerful institutional lobby that can block the real solution for places like Jawalke: training villagers like Sarubai Salve and Babai Sathe to do all these things.

"Doctors promote medical care because that's where the money is," says Raj Arole. "We promote health." The distinction is crucial to Arole, 75, a doctor himself, and the founder, along with his wife, Mabelle (who died in 1999), of the program, known as Jamkhed, that trained Salve and Sathe. The Aroles graduated top in their class from one of India's most prestigious medical schools, Christian Medical College in Vellore, Tamil Nadu. "They were trying to impose an education that would make you a good doctor in France or Germany," says Arole. But the Aroles had a different goal: to promote health among the poorest of the poor. They worked at a mission hospital, then did their residencies and studied public health in the United States.

In 1970 the Aroles returned to India and established the Comprehensive Rural Health Project in Jamkhed, a small city that is about an eight-hour drive east of Mumbai. They chose the location—not far from where Raj Arole grew up—because it was in one of the poorest parts of the state, frequently drought-stricken almost to the point of famine. There was no local industry or train service. People stayed alive by cultivating small patches of sorghum. Irrigation consisted of asking the gods for rain.

When they came to Jamkhed, the Aroles started a small hospital in an abandoned veterinary clinic. A hospital was necessary to treat complicated illnesses and emergencies, and it gave the project political support and credibility. It also brought in fees from patients who could pay. (Those fees, together with donations, contribute the bulk of Jamkhed's $500,000 annual budget for their village work even today.) But

Doctors promote medical care because that's where the money is. We promote health.

the Aroles knew that curative medicine could do very little for the poor. They needed to emphasize preventive medicine, and bring it to the villages. So they decided to engage the villagers themselves. A village health worker, Arole says, can take care of 80 percent of the village's health problems, because most are related to nutrition and to the environment. Infant mortality is actually three things: chronic starvation, diarrhea, and respiratory infections. For all three, you do not need doctors. "Rural problems are simple," Arole says. "Safe drinking water, education, and poverty alleviation do more to promote health than diagnostic tests and drugs."

When Salve and Sathe started their work in Jawalke, they were destitute. As members of the Dalit, or Untouchable, castes, they were considered nonpersons, so reviled that higher caste people would throw out food if it even touched the edge of their saris. They went barefoot in the village, as Untouchable women were not allowed to wear shoes. Sathe remembers standing for hours at the local water pump—which she could not touch—waiting for a higher caste woman to take pity on her and fill her bucket. Salve was so poor she washed her hair with mud and owned a single sari. When she laundered it, she had to stay in the river until it dried.

As the Aroles expanded their program to a hundred or more villages outside Jamkhed, they encouraged villages to select women from lower castes. "An educated woman likely comes from a high caste—she may not [want to] work for the poorest of the poor," says Arole. The Aroles believed that empathy, knowledge of how poor people live, and willingness to work were more important than skills and prestige.

Many village health workers were completely illiterate when they began training. When Sathe first started making rounds in Jawalke, she had never attended a day of school. Salve had completed fourth grade. Sathe was married at the age of ten; Salve at two and a half. Every worker I met was married by age 13. Many had been abandoned by their husbands. Others talked about terrible beatings; Surekha Sadafule, who is 26, recounted how her husband threw her down a well after she bore him a daughter. Her parents would not allow her to come home. "You must suffer whatever he gives you," they said. "That is Indian culture."

The health workers' first task was to transform themselves, beginning with two weeks of training on Jamkhed's campus. The Aroles' daughter Shobha, 47, a doctor who is now associate director of the program, conducted some of the training. "I would ask, 'What's your name?' and they would say the village they come from and their caste. They had no self-identity," she says.

"They wouldn't look into your eyes or talk to you. They didn't even feel a woman has intelligence." Shobha's mother would ask the women, "Who is more intelligent—a woman or a rat?" "A rat," they would say. Shobha had the women practice saying their names in front of a mirror. She asked them, "Who is the one person who will never leave you?" Then they would walk behind a curtain to be confronted by the mirror. The training boosted their self-confidence. "Everyone can give technical knowledge," says Shobha. "What makes it successful is time spent building up their confidence." Training is an ongoing campaign: Every Tuesday many of the women return for two days to discuss problems in their villages, review what they learned the previous week, and tackle a new subject, such as heart disease. The women sleep on the floor under one enormous blanket they sewed together from small ones.

The health workers did not become village authorities instantly. It took months or years for a village to start listening, a process helped along by medical successes, such as delivering a high-caste woman's baby or curing a child's fever. The women also have backing from a mobile

An educated woman likely comes from a high caste—she may not [want to] work for the poorest of the poor.

team—a nurse, paramedic, social worker, and sometimes a doctor—who visit each village every week in the beginning, then less and less often. The mobile team sees the hardest cases and reinforces the authority of the village health worker. Sadafule told me that she and the mobile team went to the house of a high-caste woman in her village. As the caste system requires, the woman made tea for the visitors, but not for Sadafule—an Untouchable. "The social worker put the cup in my hand," Sadafule said. She had prescribed medicine, but the high-caste woman didn't trust her, and asked the nurse the same question. The nurse confirmed the prescription and asked Sadafule to take the medicine back out of her bag and give it to the woman.

Villages with Jamkhed-trained health workers were gradually transformed by their presence. After three or so years, these villages started to look very different from their neighbors. Compared with the misery of the 1970s and 1980s in rural India, there has been some progress even in villages that Jamkhed does not reach: More women are postponing marriage until 18, the use of contraception has reduced family size, and more girls are attending school. But much has not changed. In the village of Kharda, nine miles from Jawalke, wastewater runs in open rivulets. Piles of cow dung swarm with flies. Children have frequent diarrhea, vomiting, and fevers. Some educated young people say they no longer believe old superstitions, but many told me they would rush a snakebite victim to the temple, not the hospital.

By contrast, Jamkhed's successes are dramatic. Thirty-eight years after its founding, the program has trained health workers in 300 villages. Among those that have been in the program for more than a few years, the traditional scourges—childhood diarrhea, pneumonia, neonatal deaths, malaria, leprosy, maternal

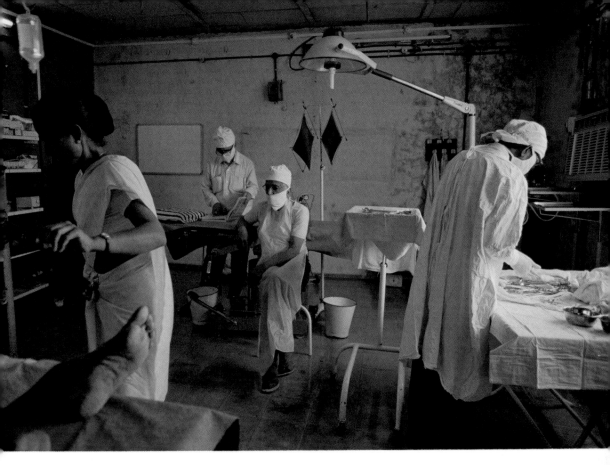

Operating on a financial shoestring, a surgical team at the Jamkhed project's only hospital can't rely upon state-of-the-art equipment. But this facility still handles everything from hip replacements to ruptured bowels. Having a hospital as part of the program helps bolster village health workers' credibility.

tetanus, tuberculosis—have virtually vanished. Jamkhed villages have far higher rates of vaccination and an infant mortality rate of 22 per 1,000 births, less than half the average for rural Maharashtra. Almost half of all Indian children under age three are malnourished, while in Jamkhed villages there are not enough cases to register. In rural Maharashtra, 56 percent of births are attended by a health worker, compared with 99 percent in Jamkhed villages.

The transformation goes beyond health. In an area once nearly bald of trees, participating villagers have planted millions, and most residents have kitchen gardens that produce spinach, papaya, and other fruits and vegetables. All Jamkhed villages have clean water, and many have pipes carrying it to a pump in every backyard. Most houses have soak pits, a simple drainage system that eliminates standing wastewater.

Sathe and Salve have organized eight women's groups in Jawalke that make these changes happen. They taught members business skills and started a loan pool—everyone ponies up a few rupees, which are lent to one person at a time so she can buy dried fish to sell or goats to raise. When we visited Jawalke, the current campaign was installing toilets. Only 85 of the village's 240 houses had one, and Sathe was trying to organize workdays to get everyone to dig drainage and install toilets at once.

Perhaps the hardest territory to colonize has been inside people's heads, where superstition and stigma prevailed. To villagers in the Jamkhed area, disease came from the gods. When a new mother died from tetanus because a dirty instrument was used to cut the umbilical cord, no one would take care of the child, says Salve. "People said the mother would become a ghost and take the child away." There were superstitions surrounding basic nutrition: Pregnant women were not supposed to eat very much, and new mothers would wait several days before starting to breast-feed. And sufferers of certain diseases, like tuberculosis and leprosy, knowing full well they'd be shunned by their neighbors, didn't dare to openly seek treatment.

Little by little, Salve and Sathe have banished such attitudes, demystifying health. Leprosy, for instance, is now treated like any other disease, which it is—leprosy is actually difficult to catch and curable with medication. The change is visible in the hands of Sakubai Gite. Now 32, she is in her sixth year as a health worker in the village of Pangulghavan. She was in her teens when leprosy took parts of her fingers before it was cured. Her hands are gnarled and deformed.

Those hands are one reason Jamkhed wanted her. "We wanted to show that a cured leprosy patient can be a village health worker," Gite said. "Today I am even permitted to deliver babies."

Discrimination against Untouchables underlies much malnutrition, neglect, and disease, but Jamkhed fights back—often mischievously. During the famine of the 1970s, Jamkhed got money to dig wells. The Untouchables, who had to live on the outskirts of their villages, begged Arole to put in two wells for each village: One for the higher caste women, and one in their neighborhood, so Untouchables could use the pump.

Arole said no. He didn't want to foster caste discrimination. He called in an American geologist with a reputation as a diviner to choose the best spot to drill. "Your job," Arole told him, "is to go around the village looking for water—but to find it only where the Untouchables live."

Soon the Untouchables had water at their doorsteps. The higher caste women, who would not normally have gone to those areas, had to break with tradition—water was more important than caste. "When 50 villages were done, people began to wonder why we were only finding water in Untouchable areas," said Arole. "But by then it was too late."

A shock awaits us back at Kale's mother's house. From the dusty light of the door we see Kale lying on a cloth in the back of the hut with a baby boy between her legs, the cord still connected. A second shock: There is a twin, not yet born.

Within minutes of Kale's agreement to go to the hospital, the driver brought the Jamkhed van around to the house. Sathe helped her in, along with a posse of women and, bizarrely, a hitchhiker in need of a ride. Kale's father and her four-year-old son sat on the floor in the front of the van. The new baby was on someone's lap.

The road was paved, but only a lane and a half wide. Each time a truck or bus came toward us, we swerved off the road. We passed bullock carts; the van's horn sounded like it was stuck in the "on" position. Salve wiped Kale's face and gave her water, and 45 minutes later we were at Jamkhed's hospital, met by three women with a gurney and whisked into the delivery room. Salve and Sathe were on either side of Kale, holding her legs and comforting her. She was still not having contractions, so a doctor gave her an injection of Pitocin to start them.

A nurse retrieved a fetal heart monitor, contained in a briefcase. Sathe held the briefcase while a nurse pushed the probe over Kale's belly. The only sound in the room was the machine's whooshing. Sathe's eyes darted around the room as the probe moved, not daring to meet Kale's. An eternity passed. There was no heartbeat.

The dead baby was a girl. Although in many Indian families a stillborn girl is no cause for sorrow, Kale felt differently. "I already had one boy," she said later, cradling her second one. "I really did want a girl." But the baby boy was healthy, born just under seven pounds.

Could the girl have been saved? Probably— if Kale had gotten a hospital sonogram at some point during the pregnancy. "We would have detected the high-risk pregnancy and had her give birth here," said Shobha. "But sometimes families are not cooperative, despite encouragement."

Seldom, however, if they are from Jawalke. In the end, the biggest health improvement brought by Sarubai Salve and Babai Sathe to this village is not the impending toilets, vaccinated children, backyard water pumps, vegetable gardens, or any other visible stuff. It is that the women of Jawalke know what constitutes a better life. And now they demand it. When Salve was at Kale's after the first baby was born, three women had gathered on the edge of the property—all young, all pregnant. They were looking for Salve for their checkups.

She nodded to them; she had her hands full; they would have to wait for now.

But tomorrow, they knew, she would come around.

Discussion Questions

- Why do you think the author begins and ends with a story that focuses on one day in the village of Jawalke? How effective do you think this introduction is?

- What rhetorical device(s) does Rosenberg use to explain why these women are so vital to the villages? How useful are those devices?

- Analyze Rosenberg's argument that the women are more effective at treating the villagers than doctors would be. How does she try to prove her point? How successful is she?

- Why does Rosenberg detail Salve and Sathe's life before they became health workers? How does this information fit with her focus on the type of care they give?

Writing Activities

- Investigate health care programs in other third world countries, and in an analytical essay compare and contrast their methods and success rates with the program in Jamkhed.

- Write copy for a 60-second commercial from a nonprofit organization trying to get funding for the program in Jamkhed. Include drawings, charts, maps, pictures, or web links to any visuals that you think would help inspire viewers to contribute.

Collaborative Activities

- Investigate the caste system in India. How did it develop? How rigid is it in the 21st century?

- Discuss in your group whether or not Indian men could become successful health workers in Indian villages. Be prepared to defend your position.

WOMEN OF SAUDI ARABIA

In "Women of Saudi Arabia" Marianne Alireza chronicles the trip she and photographer Jodi Cobb made to that country to discover what limits the government placed on women's rights. After interviewing several Saudi women, Alireza concludes that women had gained freedom from some but not all of the past restrictions.

As you read "Women of Saudi Arabia," you should consider the following questions:

- What restrictions were placed on Saudi women at the time the article was written?
- What freedoms had women gained and how had they gained them?
- How is Islamic law used to justify limits on women's rights?

Veiled to all men beyond her family, a young Bedouin woman wears the classic face covering of her people. Given only passing mention by the Koran, Islam's holy book, the veil is an ancient custom traced to India and Persia; it was adopted by Arabia's nomadic tribes, which enforced a strict code of female modesty. The tradition lives on in today's oil-rich Kingdom of Saudi Arabia—a male-dominated culture in which a man's personal and family honor depends on the conduct of females under his care.

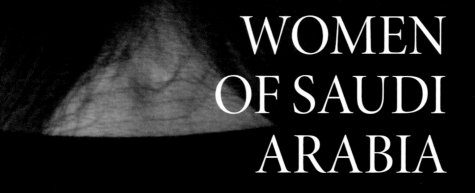

WOMEN
OF SAUDI
ARABIA

An iron fist dominates a traffic circle in Jiddah where it decorates a traffic circle. Even here, in the most worldly of Saudi Arabian cities, a woman cannot board an airplane or stay in a hotel without written permission from a male relative. And her modesty is zealously guarded by the muttawwiun—morals police armed with camel prods, who publicly shame anyone offending their sense of propriety.

SAY TO THE BELIEVING WOMEN, THAT THEY CAST DOWN THEIR EYES . . .

AND REVEAL NOT THEIR ADORNMENT . . .

AND LET THEM CAST THEIR VEILS OVER THEIR BOSOMS. . . .

Koran, Sura xxiv: 31

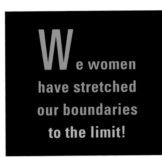
We women have stretched our boundaries to the limit!

"*Shuf, shuf,*" sang Ibtissam Lutfy, giving me a start because the words mean "See see," and she is blind. We had been talking about Arabia in the 1940s, when I went to live there as the American wife of a young Saudi. That was a time when Arabian women, bound by tradition, veiled, cloaked, segregated, often illiterate, had little say in their lives.

"Yes, those were narrow days," Ibtissam said. "But there are no more narrow days for me—and, besides, things have changed. We women have stretched our boundaries to the limit!" Now in her mid-30s, she overcame these same taboos to become a professional singer, something men didn't do 20 years ago, let alone a young girl.

Impulsively, Ibtissam invited photographer Jodi Cobb and me to a wedding in her home city of Jiddah—but telephoned next day to cancel because her father would not permit more photographs of her.

Before we left Saudi Arabia, many other women from all strata of society would make similar apologies. In the sense that nearly three-quarters of a million girls go to school in the kingdom and thousands of women have earned university degrees and play a role in the progress of the nation, lives are indeed broader. But this is still a country where the man's word is usually final, where even six-year-old girls cover their heads.

For city women like us, just about the only activity (besides living communally within the extended family) consisted of leaving our harem quarters to visit other women in theirs. Family men or male servants did the shopping. Older women ran the household, with younger women having few such duties. Yet despite this hierarchy of age, everyone belonged—even I, even before I learned to share and care as a small part of the big whole. "We love you as we love our son," were the first words I heard from my mother-in-law, Asma, and my extended family sailed me through my first Christmas with a roast turkey and gifts placed under the tree Mother had had flown in from Cairo. With wonderful sensitivity they helped me celebrate my religious

Adapted from "Women of Saudi Arabia" by Marianne Alireza: National Geographic Magazine, October 1987.

feast. Outside the walls we had little, but what we did inside the walls was live together.

> Islam is the **one thing** that **has not changed.**

Today, as if overnight on history's clock, Saudi Arabia has a new face from development, modernization, industrialization; its people adapt to change while simultaneously being educated; and there's a new reality whose meaning and direction can still not be fully assessed, particularly as concerns women, as concerns Islam.

Islam is the one thing not changed. It is the state, the moral and civil code; it is all matters big and small, ever imbued with an awareness of God's will and word. Now, though, the big and small changes unloosed over the Saudis have created a need to rethink how God's will and word apply in their world of today and to invent ingenious ways to make it all fit together.

Sunni Islam as it is practiced in Saudi Arabia has no hierarchy of priesthood, not even a formal clergy, but there is no shortage of definitive religious directives for the faithful. These emanate from a powerful body of Islamic scholars called the *ulama,* who cling tenaciously to strict puritanical tenets and moral codes and whose minds are set in archaic and traditional beliefs, particularly regarding the decency and morality of women. Public-morality committees, the regional Societies for the Preservation of Virtue and the Prevention of Vice, ensure strict compliance with religious requirements and what passes for religious requirements. Salaried morals police patrol the public domain making sure that businesses close at prayer times, that women are properly covered and observe the off-limits signs on, say, popular disco-music cassette shops, where mingling might provide a breeding ground for assignations.

The General Presidency for Girls' Education takes its top orders from men of God, keeping the threads of religion tight and binding—modernity may pad the fabric of society but not tear it.

Men, of course, go right on doing what they do, so the import for them is nowhere near what it is for women, who certainly seek no diminution of their role as Islamic women but may nonetheless perceive that role differently—especially as they learn to read and understand for themselves the legitimate rights given to them by Islam in the seventh century A.D.

In Islam the woman has a fully independent legal personality. She can inherit and own property, can divorce in certain situations, and has the same religious duties as a man: "O mankind, We have created you male and female, and appointed you races and tribes, that you may know one another Surely the noblest among you in the sight of God is the most godfearing of you" (Koran, Sura XLIX:13).

Man-created traditions and practices often denied women the rights due them, and years ago, while living the restrictive life, I often blurted to my mother-in-law, "But how can you accept this, why do you allow it to be?" She answered always, "It is our way." Well, the way has changed.

For local color, Fridays on Jiddah's corniche along Red Sea is hard to beat. Miles of sun-protected picnic areas and playgrounds line the shore where hundreds of Jiddawis *en famille* gather in their own private public spot—men, women, and children together—a notable difference from the days of men with men in public and women with women in homes.

But it is understood that being in public does not mean going public. Women's head coverings (not always over faces) stay on, and cloaks, though billowed by sea breezes, are kept firmly in place with ease and grace while ladies serve food, play with children, swing on the swings, or make the rounds on a Ferris wheel. But never mind, it's the outing that counts, so credit the government for planning and providing, and credit the change in mentality it represents.

Rural and nomadic women have always enjoyed more freedom than their city counterparts. *Badawiyyat*—Bedouin women—are still the only Saudi women driving, far from the crowds and the morals police, with pickup trucks and water rigs replacing the camel and treks to the wells on foot.

Welcomed into part of a rude complex of pens and lean-tos near Taif one day by three outgoing, pretty daughters of a goatherd, Jodi and I drank the proffered tea while they proceeded to learn as much about us as we did about them. They kept goats while their brothers went to school, and they didn't know how old they were, but they loved the Polaroid snapshots we took of them and carefully hid each one away. I wondered what ten more years would bring for them.

Ibrahim Ahmad al-Sayed, a member of the Asir governor's staff and the director of the provincial tourism department, came with his driver to take Jodi and me around the countryside near Abha one morning. Stopping at a two-in-one village—old ruins next to a living settlement—I called to an elderly village woman, "Peace be upon you!"

"And upon you be peace!"

"May we visit you?"

"Welcome, welcome," she said.

In layered village garb, some of it embroidered, some printed, some black, and no veil but a black head wrap that she tried to angle slightly over her blind eye, she led us to the second-floor sitting room of her towerlike home. Leaving our shoes at the threshold, we sat on low mats along walls featuring a painted running design and swooping electric wiring and were barely settled when to my utter surprise Ibrahim joined us and, wonder of wonders, even the driver. That would never have happened in Jiddah—certainly not in Riyadh—men strangers visiting the lady of the house.

This widowed matriarch of the al-Asiri family, with three sons in the army, kept the home, the goats, and the adjacent farm, with her daughters-in-law (who—aha!—did not appear) and seven grandchildren, four in school, three still too young.

In Riyadh we met a citified Badawiyah, Umm (mother of) Abdallah, who lives in an apartment and has a hospital technician daughter and a pharmacist son, but keeps her makeshift stall in the Bedouin market selling everything from gold, turquoise, and silver to ragtag notions and remnants of old Bedouin clothes.

We sat there on the ground with her and friends, partaking of dates and Arabic coffee served from a coffeepot that was identical in shape to the traditional brass one, but it was a thermos made of plastic. Other signs of the times are traditional *madass* (men's sandals) available now in the fine leathers of Italian shoemakers and the ultimate in veils and cloaks bearing logos and labels of famed Paris couturiers.

Umm Abdallah loved adorning herself for photographs with every possible piece of silver, but her fun and ours stopped when a male passerby shouted a protest and announced he was going for the police.

"May you be blinded and boiled in oil," Umm Abdallah shouted after him, but she scurried to hide all camera gear in Bedouin baskets, under old clothes, in an old trunk. That time the police did not come.

Women such as Umm Abdallah are only partly out of the old time. The real changes lie in the generation or so after them. Today's educated women might still wear the veil, might still be the wives and mothers they have always been, but they have become other things too.

In their ranks are teachers, computer technicians, social workers, laboratory technicians, physical fitness instructors, physicists, engineers, bankers, filmmakers. All these when the first public schools for girls weren't approved by the government until 1960!

"Thank God things have changed for us!" This not from the younger nurses at a hospital dispensary but from a widowed mother of seven (the oldest a boy of 15) just now learning to read and write in the government program for adult illiterates, *(Continued on page 68)*

(Continued from page 65) having to juggle time seeing to her children, working required hours, attending class.

She has a serious need to work, but the young girls were there because they wanted to be, succeeding over protests of family men who look on nursing as a demeaning occupation for young women. They give modern treatments, instruction, and care in the dispensary and in patients' homes, a great change from the folk medicine, cupping, and *kawi* (applying red-hot irons to the body) so prevalent before.

At King Abd al-Aziz University Hospital in Jiddah I asked Sabah Abu Znadah, coordinator of training and development, how she had gotten into nursing.

"Do you want a flowery answer or do you want the truth?" she fired back with a smile. In truth she wanted to be a physician, but she missed the college's deadline for applications. Nursing was next best. "So I went for it," she said, "and now I'll fight for it."

Most Saudi professionals we interviewed "went for it" in one way or another. Some came from traditional families whose men objected to their working—"not," said Sabah, "because they were not open-minded men or too strict, but out of fear that society would look down on them."

Many had uneducated mothers pushing daughters to achieve what they never had; others had family support all the way. "My father always told us to get an education first, because the more like us, the more others will follow," said Fatmah Yamani, chief of personnel at the university hospital. One of her colleagues said that her father is now proud of her in her profession, but initially objected so strongly that he sent her to Jordan, where she found the "too free life" uncomfortable, so she returned to sit idly at home until her father gave up and gave in.

However they made it, women who have achieved avoid doing anything that could stem the tide of advancement. They proceed quietly on their merits, wanting no backlash spoiling things for them and for the women who will come after them.

Although most work in all-female facilities, some doctors, nurses, administrators, radio announcers, journalists do work with men. Long skirts, long sleeves, head scarves are customary for women on the job. "There is no problem," said one hospital worker. "We are well accepted, get the same pay, and men here want more women in jobs, appreciating our efforts and respecting the levels of education that put us here."

"There *are* objections around the country though," said another. "Someone wrote the newspapers asking how their girls could work next to men. Then everyone waited to see what would happen and *nothing* happened. Someone must make the first step."

"Your steps seem big to me," I told the women at the hospital. "I've heard that girls consistently outdo boys in scholastic testing, and that in one graduating class girls were outnumbered thirty to one but took the top five places. How do you account for that?"

This got a laugh and then a bigger one with the reply: "That's because boys have cars, and we must stay home and study." Judging from the letters-to-the-editor columns in local newspapers, a lot of women would like to drive too, and by such means they keep asking the king for permission.

Another slant on this subject came during a later interview with a Ph. D. requesting anonymity. "As for women driving," she said, "some people talk about it, but most feel that driving here is very dangerous and initially for women would be as disastrous as when men started. Accident factor aside, it would be worse because men unaccustomed to seeing women drive would follow and bother. It would be great sport!"

Seeing young ladies running computers was enough to make one realize what inroads education has made to future directions. Thirty years ago there were only a few high schools for boys, and in 1957 the first university class consisted of only 50 young men. The class of '73 was the first to graduate women, their number no greater than the total of hospital personnel we interviewed in one day in Jiddah—a dozen!

Same spark too. When those graduates didn't find their names on the commencement program, they set up such a hue and cry that a special ceremony was arranged. Two thousand women arrived to celebrate with them, giving the affair the joyous atmosphere of a wedding when they shook the rafters with a piercing sustained ululation.

At the King Saud University College for Women in Riyadh, students wearing black cloaks are let off by car and driver at the guarded gate. Once inside they fan out in waves of brighter colors, as veils and cloaks get folded away and the black sameness becomes laughing young women in pretty frocks hurrying to classes.

Unveiled women may not be seen by their male professors, so courses are conducted via closed-circuit television, each student having her own desk set. If, as the professor speaks, the student has a question, she has only to pick up her own telephone by the TV and have direct-line access to the lecturer.

Before their own universities, women studied by correspondence, and Faiza Abdallah al-Khayyal is one who worked as liaison between professors and female students as long ago as 1969, after she received her B.A. in sociology from Vassar.

"*You* met with the professors?" I asked.

"No," she laughed, "I'd telephone them."

Even participation in modern sports—limited in public to men and boys—met initial objection from religious leaders who took exception to shorts and bare legs and claimed that televised games encouraged Saudi youth to neglect studies. The national soccer team scored well though. It won the Asia Cup in 1984.

In a two-hour luncheon with professional women, we heard of government policies for women backsliding from enlightened to

Do you want a flowery answer or do you want the truth?

more restricted; of efforts to deflate curricula to bare-bones studies geared to making better wives and mothers; of formerly productive training and study facilities shut or limited; of access to the workplace narrowing so that highly qualified women are stymied in their careers. Asking for a summing-up statement of their feelings on this, we got this cannonball response: "HELP!"

Women, their faces exposed but their heads covered, appear occasionally on television as newscasters and special program presenters. Samar Fatany used to be one of them. She is now on radio shedding light on Saudi laws and culture for English-speaking listeners.

Educated abroad, Samar wants to prove to foreigners that Saudis are not any different. She sees some of the same adverse effects of change in her own society as are seen elsewhere—the misuse of money, time, and leisure. She is so concerned that in off-hours she runs, from her home, a club for children and homemaking classes for young wives and mothers.

Remembering the strict segregation of the past, I am still amazed at mixed society in public. Married couples can be seen shopping together, dining tête-à-tête in public in a hotel or restaurant, but still cherished and jealously guarded is their personal privacy. Increased one-on-one sharing as husband and wife, as parents, may be due to a certain fragmentation of the extended family, with the added factor that some wives are now as educated as their spouses.

Private groups mix too. Couples join good friends in each other's homes with astonishing frequency—three or four times a week—making a shared enjoyable little world within the bigger confining one around them. They enjoy weekends together, travel together, share joys and problems in support of each other, and their young folk associate freely—all forming a circle of friends that becomes a new extended family.

Children and teenagers in these situations obviously enjoy freedom and activities unknown where the conservatism of the people keeps life within traditional traces, where even very small girls wear the black cloak and head covering, and the scene of a hundred or so of them frolicking on paths home from school is startling.

Marriage is something for which many now wait longer than before, wanting an education first. This is not to say that pressures to marry are not still there. "Our Girls and the Right Path" was the subject of a seminar in Jiddah in 1986 where Saudi scholar and Professor of Islamic Culture Ahmad Jamal indicated that marriage is a woman's primary obligation and takes precedence over the pursuit of learning. Unless, that is, a husband agrees informally or by legal prenuptial writ to her continuing studies after marriage.

Just getting married poses problems for some because of prohibitively high dowries and excessive outlays for celebrations. One sheikh representing ten tribes attempted to set dowry limits in his region when they reached 160,000 Saudi riyals ($42,000). He proposed maximums of 10,000 riyals plus some jewelry and a gold watch for a virgin, and 5,000 for a divorcee or a widow. One news report in 1986 listed the nationwide average as 100,000 riyals.

A Muslim can have four wives legally at a time if—a big if—he can give each wife equal material goods and equal time. So monogamy is by far the norm, although divorce rates are on the rise. With a man allowed to divorce his wife without stating reasons, there can be instances where the divorcée faces dire problems. Women can divorce too, given certain reasons outlined in the Koran, but instituting such action in a male-dominated society can be as difficult as trying to counteract any unfair conditions unilaterally imposed on a woman and children by an uncooperative or vengeful husband.

Learning to read may lessen the incidence of such situations, as women come to

> **I**slam never said that women should not be educated. The Koran says **learning is incumbent** upon male and female.

know what Islam truly wants of them and for them. Along with those individual rights to inherit, own property, and divorce, Islam also has provisions for prenuptial contracts and deferred dowries (contingency amounts set aside for the ifs and whens), and no infringement is brooked of what is lawfully theirs. Women have always owned property and handled their moneys, even before education and from behind the veil, and as the country grew and developed, so did women's investments and holdings, and this gave rise to the proliferation of women's banks.

With all that women *can* do, there are things even today that they cannot do, such as board airline flights without written permission from a male family member or check into any of the kingdom's hotels without a letter in hand from a male relative or official sponsor permitting them to do so, and this also applies to foreign women.

One distinguished gentleman friend regards the travel restriction as a source of shame and embarrassment when he or one of his five brothers must sign for their beloved mother when she leaves on a jaunt. "When our father died," he said, "she single-handedly raised us, did for us, taught us, shaped us into what we are today, and after all this we have to sign for *her*. How demeaning!"

At the King Saud College for Women, Jodi and I listened to a cracking good debate:

"Islam never said that women should not be educated. The Koran says learning is incumbent upon male and female."

"But what does one do about educated women here whose only concern is children, the soap opera, the fat in the diet?"

"Well, I am educated and can give the best of both worlds."

"And I don't like the condescending attitude of some who say, 'You poor women here, you can't drive; you poor women, you can't talk to a man; you poor this or that.' I wouldn't change for millions, and who asked them? It's my world and I accept it."

"Well yes, but in our society we *do* have some things that need to be changed and others, like driving, that we'd enjoy but that are not the most important things in life. And I can wait until society is ready. It is a part of our life that change is coming. It might take longer, it might take shorter, but we are hoping for the best for our society, within our religion, within our morals, within our readiness to foresee and digest change. Because then it will be for the better."

Inshallah.

Discussion Questions

- Why does Alireza begin with an anecdote about Ibtissam Lutfy, a Saudi Arabian woman who subsequently invited Alireza to her wedding? How does this story fit in with the rest of the article? Do you think it is an effective opening to the article?

- Why do you think Alireza includes personal details about her past and her faith in the article? What effect do these details have on her overall presentation of Saudi women?

- How do the quotes from the *Koran* that Alireza includes in the article provide supporting evidence for her claims?

- What do you think the author's attitude is toward the changes that had been made in regard to women's rights at the time she wrote the article?

Writing Activities

- Conduct research on how women in Saudi Arabia are treated today. Write an analytical essay exploring the changes that have been made to their status and rights and the traditions concerning their roles in society that have not changed.

- Put yourself in the role of an activist for women's rights in Saudi Arabia. Prepare a speech calling for the equal treatment of women that you will present to a governmental hearing on the subject of women's rights. As part of your argument, you will need to address traditional notions of a woman's place as expressed by political and religious leaders.

- The author wonders why Saudi women do not try to fight against restrictions placed on them. Write an essay that considers the possible reasons women would rather embrace tradition than fight for equal rights.

Collaborative Activities

- Discuss how Figure 7.2 represents life for Saudi women during the time that the article was written. After doing research on current laws concerning women's equality in Saudi Arabia, determine whether this photograph can still be considered an accurate symbol of their oppression.

- Decide whether or not sanctions should be brought against countries that do not grant equal rights to women. Be prepared to defend your position to the class.

WOMEN AT WORK

La Verne Bradley documents the surge of women in the American workplace during World War II in her article, "Women at Work." She details the various jobs the women held and how successful they were at them.

As you read "Women at Work," you should consider the following questions:

- What types of jobs did women hold during World War II in and outside the military?
- How quickly did women learn new skills?
- How were they treated by their male coworkers?

At the Touch of Her Finger, This Monster Hydropress Molds Metal Liberator Parts
The inside underpart of the huge hydraulic press is hard rubber. As it comes slowly down, the rubber pad presses and shapes sheets of metal to the die at the bottom. The press is used only for mass-production jobs and can stamp out several different small parts at once.

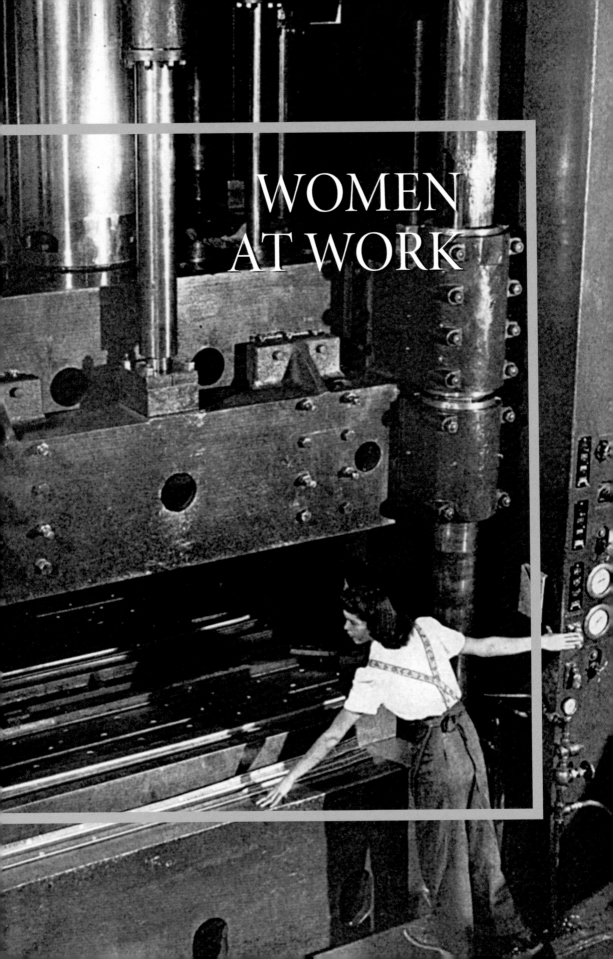

WOMEN
AT WORK

No Time to Prink in the Mirrorlike Tail Assembly of a Liberator
About a third of the country's aircraft workers are women. Many jobs they do as well as men; some they do better. Riveting, a kind of needle point in metals, is one of women's standout operations.

WOMEN WORKED IN A
WIDER VARIETY OF FIELDS AND INDUSTRIES
THAN EVERY BEFORE IN WORLD WAR II. WOULD WOMEN'S RIGHTS BE WHERE THEY ARE TODAY WITHOUT WAR HAVING PLANTED THE SEEDS?

The balance of power rests in women's hands. Literally.

Behind the whine of sawmills and roar of blast furnaces, the hammer of arsenals and thunder of machine shops—in shipyards, factories, foundries, slaughterhouses, and laboratories—women are manipulating the machinery of war.

They work the giant hydropresses and stamping mills whose heavy weights are constantly pounding, pressing, shaping, disgorging the materials of battle. They operate drop hammers, punch presses, turret lathes, milling machines. They hold rivet guns, blow-torches, drills, files, micrometers, templates, and test tubes.

For three years they have laid down blueprints, welded seams, and picked up battle gear, put it on wheels, and carried it for proving. Then they've inspected, tested, proved it, and delivered it for war.

At the same time, they've worked to keep their homes or set up new ones under makeshift conditions in strange places.

About a third of America's manpower today is womanpower. That's more than one out of every three women of working age in the United States. Of the millions handling the big

> The balance of power rests in women's hands. Literally.

tools and machines of industry, one-half are estimated to be there only because of the war.

Approximately one-fourth of the 16,500,000 women holding jobs in the spring of this year were not even interested in such work in 1940! Many had never seen a factory, never hammered a tack, never worked before at anything outside the home.

Reports of the Women's Bureau, Department of Labor, disclose the amazing variety of jobs women hold.

In Aircraft Production

A week before Pearl Harbor you could walk through the factory rooms of any aircraft company in the country and rarely find a woman on the production line. They were a fraction of one percent of the total labor force.

Two years later, 475,000 women made up nearly 35 percent of the industry. More than 45 percent of the workers for Douglas Aircraft are women. And in the first 12 months that the output of B-17's was doubled, nearly half

Adapted from "Women at Work" by La Verne Bradley: National Geographic Magazine, August 1944.

the men at Boeing necessarily were replaced by completely inexperienced women.

"Long before there was a manpower shortage we began to employ women on the assembly line," said Glenn L. Martin, builder of famous fighting and patrol bombers. "We were one of the first aircraft companies to employ women in mechanical capacities.

"However, it was an eminently successful experiment. There will always be a place for the skilled woman worker in the aircraft industry. Many jobs she performs as well as men, and some she performs better.

"Today, approximately 35 percent of the productive workers building Martin combat ships are women. Soon we look forward to seeing this number vastly increased, as more and more of our younger men are called up for military duty.

"We have women helping design our planes in the Engineering Department, building them on the production line, operating almost every conceivable type of machinery, from rivet guns to giant stamp presses.

"The presence of so many women has had an excellent effect upon production. They have set production records that are a challenge to men, and there's something about a woman beating a man at his own machine that he just cannot stand".

"Bombs Away, Beautiful!"

As I walked into the shop where the giant *Mars* was built and where great PBM-3's were lined up for final assembly, I heard a man's voice calling out from the cavern of a huge wing, "Bombs away, beautiful!"

Straddled over a truss in the bomb bay, he was checking shackle releases as a girl down in the depths of the ship fired an electric gun and kept tab on the panel flashing salvo signals—single bombs, bombs in sequence, wham, bombs away.

Usually two girls do this alone, calling back and forth by interphone from one remote end of the ship to the other. I watched them swing up through compartment hatches and scramble over spars and beams like cats.

Martin has also an all-girl test crew, which went into action for the first time on an icy morning this last December. They had put in months of training for one of the most crucial jobs in the business, the final ground testing and adjusting of every functioning part of a patrol bomber. Engine, instruments, controls—theirs is the final check before men take it aloft.

Through acres of bombers and chopped-up parts of bombers, silver, brown, and green, we made our way from one roaring assembly line to another. At one point we stopped to speak to a small taffy blonde, wearing a blue hair ribbon and sitting in the midst of hammering machinery, her feet propped up on a bench, reading a book.

It was her lunch hour and the manual, *Pneudraulic Power Machine and Riveters*. One of half a million housewives who had never been in a factory, she suddenly figured a couple of years ago that maybe the talents of her toolmaker father might be developed in her. They were.

Occasionally you find a woman such as Anne Hollman, and you don't forget that she is 46 and helps make one of the hottest fighter planes in the Army. She is the only woman flash welder in the East. And she is an Amazon.

In the last war she was a machine operator in a knitting mill; then she did housework for 20 years. Now she is back, master of a difficult trade and proud of her skill, towering over her bench by the hour as she stands welding ends onto control rods for Republic Thunderbolts.

In one section the foreman had said, "When the first woman is sent to my shop, send my release with her."

Some months later, I mentioned a few of the usual objections to women in industry—57 percent of man's strength, 68 percent of his resistance to fatigue, etc.—and this same foreman defended them hotly.

He specifically pointed out the girl who was turning out five assembly units to her male predecessor's two.

Womanpower in Shipyards

In 1939 there were 36 women employed in American shipyards.

Two years ago when I saw women working on destroyers and submarines and in the machine shops at the Mare Island Navy Yard and on tankers and other ships around San Francisco Bay, I was told that there were jobs which women could never do—shipfitting, for instance, and chipping, and handling the big cranes.

Kaiser put them on the big cranes and now they handle them with ease, swinging giant steel arms out over yards to pick up whole bulkheads or afterpeaks and lift them to the ways. Shipfitting and chipping, along with dozens of other all-male jobs, they've taken in stride.

Thousands of women are doing such things as welding and riveting. About the only thing they do not do is heavy lifting.

It is illegal in some States. But in many cases, even these operations have been broken down to permit women to handle them.

It took 175 tons of blueprint, 4,300,000 feet of welding, and 3,830,000 man-and-woman days to build the U.S.S. *Missouri.* Every Navy craft produced takes proportional figures. And enough preliminary and supplementary work to make you wonder if anything else is going on anywhere.

At the David Taylor Model Basin in Maryland, where the Navy experiments with new ship designs and tests scale models of both Army and Navy craft, I found Dr. Avis Borden working in the structural mechanics division developing methods of calibrating

One of half a million housewives who had never been in a factory, she suddenly figured a couple of years ago that maybe the talents of her toolmaker father might be developed in her. They were.

underwater explosion gages. She had received her degree in physics from the University of Michigan in 1938, but she had never had a chance to use it in such important work. Now her findings have been put to official use.

In another section women were taking readings on marine propellers in a variable-pressure water tunnel. In engineering and drafting rooms they were making drawings, calculating water and pressure effects, and performing intricate mathematical computations connected with naval architecture.

A Delicate Aquatic Test

Out in the damp, cavernous chamber which holds the 963-foot-long water basin, we boarded the big carriage which hauls ship models through the water channel at speeds from 18 to only 0.03 knots.

It looks like a small cantilever bridge moving through the air, but it is so delicately built that it can maintain any desired speed at a constant value within one-hundredth of a knot while following the actual curvature of the earth. Two girls in blue jeans were driving it.

Results of runs for the 20-foot model of an aircraft carrier being tested were recorded on dynamometers and translated onto charts being plotted by other women at desks which ride with the carriage. These women aren't scientists. They are just average girls, trained swiftly to do vital jobs.

At a naval gun factory women at big profiling machines were turning out rotating pans for 16-inch guns. They were working light and heavy lathes, milling machines, drill presses, thread grinders; making sears, breechblocks, and hundreds of other gun mechanisms. They were greasing giant gun barrels and painting others for battle.

A Beauty Operator Takes to Machines

Dressed in blue safety slacks and caps and stepping over huge guns lying about on the floor, or linking arms together to go to lunch, they looked almost like Rockettes against a supercolossal stage set.

The shop supervisor, who has been with the big guns since 1912, had to be shown that slight girls, such as the former beauty operator on the Keller profiler, could handle these machines.

They are trained on the job here, and trained fast. One girl had two hours' instruction on a machine, went to work, and the next day in an emergency broke in another girl. There is little difference between an inexperienced woman and an inexperienced man in this work.

And there *are* some "natural" women mechanics. "Like Joan," said the supervisor, pointing to a girl working over a big hydraulic shaper, "who should have been a boy. Except that she's better than most of them." Joan was trimming a bore for a 6-inch anti-aircraft gun to a tolerance of .001. She said she had always loved machines, but never had had a chance to get her hands on anything like *this* before.

Women physicists and engineers in the Acoustics and Special Problems Division of the Naval Ordnance Laboratory at the Washington Navy Yard have come about as close as any women to going to sea with the Navy.

They've worked on ships tied at docks. They have also gone with officers and men on field assignments to Key West, New London, and Miami. They've knocked down many precedents, and their male co-workers have discovered an important thing—they get through red tape faster.

One yard officer almost let a girl go to sea to take recordings, but the ship's skipper wouldn't break precedent.

Women are doing men's jobs for the army too.

At Narragansett Bay two girls worked on the water front in a trailer laboratory, but for their offshore tests the Army had to take them to sea in Coast Artillery boats. At the Key West Sound School, Navy men would go out by day to make sea tests, and the girl physicist they took down from the Washington research group would wait and work with them over analyses at the base by night.

You Wash My Shirt, I'll Iron Yours

When they first reported to different naval stations for scientific research, listed, the way the Navy does, as A. Axon or G. Irish, women were usually met with astonishment. It was a crisis of accommodations unless there were waves aboard. At one base A. Axon finally agreed to iron an officer's shirts if he would wash hers in the all-male laundry room.

Women working in high explosives is not new, but it is still an electrifying thing to watch. At the Bellevue Naval Magazine, a healthy distance downriver from the Navy Yard, we found women in steel-barricaded rooms measuring and loading pom-pom mix, lead azide, TNT, tetryl, and fulminate of mercury.

Most of them were colored. They seemed delightfully blase as they passed the stuff along. Some would wink or give a big grin as we poked in their booths. But they treat powder with respect. They know by training that any snip of it could blow them to flinders.

I asked the officer if their temperament—their lack of nerves, say—had anything to do with their being here in such numbers.

"No," he said, "they like that extra six cents an hour hazard pay. This is one of the few jobs in industry which has a waiting list of applications."

Different loading operations were strung along different weirdly grouped assembly lines. On one line they would be loading tetryl leadins for bomb fuses, or delay elements containing small cells of black powder, or mercury fulminate and lead azide for detonators.

In small steel booths others would receive an element through a hole in the wall, put in the measured milligrams of powder and pass it quietly through an opposite hole to the next booth for another cautious twist, or tap, or turn.

The workers are frisked every morning for matches. During smoking periods they walk way off from danger areas to where electric cigarette lighters are provided in safety zones.

The *Iowa* and women were launched the same day at the Brooklyn Navy Yard, when the first 19 came in as "mechanic learners." There are several thousand now, and many are rated machine operators, skilled welders, ship-fitters, and supervisors.

One of the first 19 heads them all today. She took us through mold loft, fabricating sections, and shipfitting departments with the air of an old hand.

"It's really simple to build a ship," she explained. "You get your plan, cut out your pattern, prefabricate it, fit it together, and launch it. Men have always made such a job of it!"

She knew what each yellow streak on the big steel sheets indicated, where they would go, how they should be fitted. She explained air hammers, calking tools, and electrodes; how they burned out holes for pipes, cables, hatches; how they chipped off excess stock from steel plates, welded seams, flushed rivets.

Beginning in the mold loft, she had climbed around on hands and knees, working over blueprints, laying out templates, tracing patterns along body plans on the floor; then on through riveting, welding, shipfitting.

They used mostly college girls in the mold loft at first, until they found that almost any average girl has aptitude for pattern making. They're all over the place now, bending over plotting tables, crawling over loft decks, moving about in similar clothes like blue beetles.

In the great shipfitting department we walked in a world of giants. Everything was big—noise, and space, and parts of ships.

Blue oxygen flashes would light up remote corners to outline human figures bent like small parentheses around huge steel plates; or golden sparks would suddenly sheer out from a chipper's gun; or sprays of silvery molten metal would touch off another dark section until you could feel the very depth and height of it.

Stooped over acetylene torches or hidden behind steel helmets visored to protect them from the intense light of arcs, women in bulky leather pants and jackets labored feverishly over welds and seams.

A Variety of Army Jobs

Women are doing men's jobs for the Army, too.

For the Air Forces they teach cadets to fly, dispatch bombers and fighters at busy air bases, repair planes, and do sheet-metal work.

For the Army Service Forces, which alone employs more civilian industrial labor than any economic empire in the country, they manufacture explosives, load bombs, test parachutes, inspect war plants, and handle giant tooling machines, cranes, tractors, furnaces, compressors.

They mend shoes and tanks. They drive convoy trucks for the Signal Corps and locomotives for the Ordnance Department; they make uniforms for the Quartermaster Corps, and count fish for the Army Engineers.

They are laborers, machinists, electricians, tinsmiths, pipe fitters, architects, chemists, surveyors, attorneys.

As the Army Engineers moved into combat work, thousands of women poured in to help with the jobs left behind—river and harbor work, navigation and flood control, surveying, designing, building—jobs formerly done only by Army engineers or their civilian male assistants. Today 29 percent of the 84,000 civilians behind the Army Engineers are women.

They have measured the depth of the Columbia River for charting and dredging; they operate radios to Mississippi River boats. They work with the Army in the field, computing soil erosion, levee seepage, silting; charting evaporation rates and wave action on breakwaters.

They have followed the Engineers almost everywhere except overseas. One girl has driven an Army truck for three years through all kinds of weather to run mail to them in Alaska.

Dr. Mary Engle Pennington, the Quartermaster General's consultant on food handling, has ridden in the caboose of refrigerator trains, in the bottom hold of cargo vessels, and waded knee-deep in eggshells studying improved ways to get food to the Army.

Women of the Transportation Corps handle more than 200 types of Army vehicles at the gigantic shipping pools at ports of embarkation. They check these vehicles mechanically, wash and drain them, pack parts in grease, tape and shellac others against sea spray. And they get the ships in shape to carry them. They weld, clean, paint, carpenter, plumb, and check electric systems.

They help move freight from trains to ships, run trucks down dark narrow passages of warehouses and piers, operate fork lifts to stack and unstack tons of equipment, manipulate big cranes to place tanks and guns in loading position.

On a siding at the Aberdeen Proving Ground in Maryland, we found captured German tanks were lined up with other equipment returned from the front for testing. Yellow turrets and hulls were spattered with names, dates, messages from the boys who reached them first—"Cpl. J. Hanson—Naples—November 2, 1943."

> These aren't the glamour jobs—but they're collateral to victory.

Then scrawled across a gun mount—"Why the hell don't you boys come over and pick up your own equipment?"

Aberdeen is the world's largest proving ground. All the fighting tools of the Army, and some for the Navy, are put to test here—bombs, shells, guns, bullets, trucks, tanks, even paints and lubricants.

There is a feel of war about it so thick it penetrates. If you forget it for a minute, a giant gun will boom in the distance, windows will rattle and buildings shake, and you'll feel it through the soles of your shoes. And flares will drop over in the next field from test planes whining high overhead.

Music Amid the Noise

They said women's nerves couldn't stand the noise of the big guns, that their frames wouldn't take it. Women ordnance workers can stand anything.

In the shop at the Frankford Arsenal where casings for gun shells are made, the industrial crescendo of all America seemed to me to reach its peak. It was a different kind of noise from the big guns, but equally shattering. It was steady and penetrating and mixed—the thunder of giant stamping machines, the pounding of drop hammers, the whish of boiling water, and the ringing of bumping metal, all run together like the big, noisy climax of "Götterdämmerung."

"We have music, too," said the major. I couldn't hear it, though passing workers seemed to be whistling to something. After picking noises apart, like going through apples, I finally made out the faint strain of a march, and then I noticed an amazing thing. Hands threw levers, loaded conveyers, and whipped from shell to shell in rhythm. It was fantastic.

Women work faster on these jobs than on any I saw anywhere in any industry. It happens to be that kind of work.

One Can Almost Feel the Heat and Hear the Bark of This Aircraft Gun Test
The girl pulls the rope trigger and stands away while a 20-mm. machine gun is given a breakdown test at Aberdeen (Maryland) Proving Ground. Composition wall blocks are sound-absorbent and fire-resistant. Girl fires until gun breaks down or the officer whistles.

Mountains of flat brass disks would dissolve as they were grabbed and rolled under stamps and came out smaller disks; then under another press which stretched them to shell cases, and on through 25 operations in a matter of split seconds.

At the 40-mm. tapering operation, which gives shell cases that indented curve, long belts fed a chain of straight brass cylinders to the big press. Women would snatch them from the belt and slip them under the hammer, then grab them off and set them in moving conveyer cups, all in a single pendulum motion.

Hundreds of women were doing the same thing for different-sized shell cases on different-sized machines. Thousands of hands and fingers seemed to be in constant motion, back and forth, as stamping machines moved ceaselessly up and down, up and down. Soapy steam from scalding tubs filled the air with an eerie mist.

It seemed like pretty rough, hurried work for stuff that should be so infinitely accurate. They told me that a woman worker with a son in the Army had come to them recently with the same question. She had a shell case in her hand that had been dented somehow. They took her carefully through each department, past correcting machines, testing gages, and final inspections until she could return to her job with confidence.

Men said there were jobs that our women wouldn't do—hot, heavy, unglamorous jobs in steel mills and oil refineries and on railroads. They are in all of them today.

We saw women laying out sheet metal in a broiling summer sun, perspiration rolling down the dirty collars of their shirts. We watched them heaving sand on railroad tracks in temperatures below zero.

We sickened to the smells of chemical laboratories filled with women preparing medicines, anesthetics, explosives. I came away wondering how they could stand hour after hour under the screaming, thundering noise of assembly lines.

Hundreds of thousands of war-working women have taken their families to new homes, thrown up feverishly near aircraft plants, shipyards, arsenals, mills, and mines. Nurseries have had to be built for their children.

Employers have added work incentives and securities of ingenious description—counselors, nurses, gymnasiums, clubs, uniforms, rest periods, hot food, music. Some factories have become worlds of their own with "night finals" published by the plant for every shift.

This isn't always the case, of course, even in war. The sister of a famous author, working for a big company in New England, said, "It's still a long run on a cold day to the women's annex, tacked onto an all-male plant."

Flagpole Painters and Junk Sorters

In Kansas City a woman paints flagpoles. New Orleans has a couple of women trash collectors; Lawrence, Massachusetts, three junk sorters. And an appeal has been made to the women of Chicago "weighing more than 200 pounds who enjoy outdoor work and have no objection to the aroma of garbage."

Women in slaughterhouses are brain pickers, belly graders, stomach scrubbers, sweetbread pullers, and vein pumpers. They also have a spice girl.

You've seen women cabbies, bus drivers, trolley motormen, and messengers. You've landed at airports and watched them load baggage, call flights, control traffic. In Denver a girl in the glass tower sometimes directs a plane a minute on the runways while monitoring four radio circuits, a battery of telephones, and the public-address system.

They are also milkmen, postmen, firemen, street cleaners, and traffic cops. Ten policewomen patrol the Boston Common and sections of that city's entertainment arcas.

Thousands of newly trained women are keeping telephone lines open, working through the night, making quick decisions which may affect the heart of a home or a big war contract. It takes 12,000 calls to build one bomber, 87,000 to build a submarine.

These aren't the glamour jobs—but they're collateral to victory. As I write there is still a bus parked on a downtown street in San Diego with the grim sign: "Just one of many—idle for lack of drivers." And people crowd and struggle to reach the busy Navy docks and aircraft factories.

Into war plants and research laboratories have poured women geologists; physicists; meteorologists; aeronautical, radio, and electrical engineers. Women scientists are studying and experimenting with the headline materials of the age—cures for strange diseases, synthetic rubber, experimental lubricants, radar. Many are actively famous; others have brought their talents and learning out of retirement to apply them to war research.

At the University of Rochester, Dr. Frieda Robscheit-Robbins, who assisted in the research which led to the Nobel prize-winning discovery of treatment for pernicious anemia, has dropped her peacetime studies to work on a substitute for blood plasma.

In less than four years the Government alone has trained more than 2,000,000 women for war jobs.

In Plastics and Electronics

Women chemists, swathed in gauze masks, run tests in plastics and resins in the laboratories of the vast Monsanto Chemical empire. They have entered a no woman's land here in one of the biggest chemical companies in the world. The Hercules Powder Company has women Ph.D.'s experimenting with explosives.

At the Mellon Institute of Industrial Research, in Pittsburgh, the staff of women chemists has jumped 500 percent since 1941. The first woman to receive an engineering degree from Carnegie Tech is a metallographist for Westinghouse Electric & Manufacturing Company. Another Westinghouse engineer is a girl of 26 who is working in electronics research. She read her first paper last year before the American Institute of Electrical Engineers—"Skin Effect in Bimetallic Conductors."

Westinghouse is a conspicuous case of the need for skilled technicians, particularly in the field of radio and electricity, which has lost thousands of men to the Army Signal Corps. It is training dozens of women electrical engineers at Carnegie Tech.

RCA has sponsored 70 women engineering aides through Purdue to supplement its staff of graduate women radio engineers already working in vital international communications. Aircraft plants, shipyards, tooling industries—they've all set up schools for training women to replace skilled men.

In less than four years the Government alone has trained more than 2,000,000 women for war jobs. Working within industry, in schools, and on farms, it has taught them to build, design, analyze, plow. At the 200 colleges operating under the War Training program, 235,000 women have been trained for technical or professional jobs in war industries.

In the two years ending December, 1943, the Army trained almost 500,000 civilian women for jobs with the industrial, maintenance, service and supply units of the fighting forces.

At war's end, the country will emerge with a vast pool of skilled, semiskilled, and professional women.

All This, and Railroading, Too!

The very bigness and heaviness and dirtiness of railroading have kept it a man's business in this country. Like timber and steel, it was an industry of studied jobs which took skill, stomach, and usually strength. Men dominated them monastically.

It was one of the last to go over to the use of women in all-male capacities. The industry itself has always had a longer list of jobs which women could *not* do than any other.

One by one, they have entered every sacred precinct of yard and line. Old-timers have watched them with astonishment, sometimes with hostility. They are beginning to lay bets now on how long it will be before "some woman" takes 856 on its big run.

In this case, it will be some time. Locomotive engineers usually work up from firemen, and that's one job women aren't doing.

Grooming and servicing, this is mean work—but women are doing it. A big engine steams into its stall streaked with soot, grease, and smoke. They wipe it down like a lathery, muddy race horse. They put out the fire, remove the ashes, blast off the grease with live steam and chemicals, fill the sand dome, lubricate it, shine it.

Somewhere it has dropped off its grimy cars. Other women get these to clean and polish.

They pack journal boxes, operate turntables, and check cars, which means keeping track of all those numbers you see on freights (a mistake could raise havoc with a shipment of war goods); they paint, cut scrap, and handle signals and switches from coast to coast.

Those women you've seen along the track with shovels are section hands edging the ballast, burning grass and weeds, checking rails and ties. They grease switches, de-ice them in winter, and some I heard along a Pennsylvania track one January morning had even learned to speak the language.

There are women baggagemen in stations, and brakemen, flashing lanterns as you've seen thousands of men in pin-striped overalls doing all your life. Women trainmen are helping conductors, women cooks are in galleys where swaying trains and hot stoves have never permitted them before.

It takes all kinds of women to run a war. The women of the railroads are a good index of what literally keeps the wheels rolling. You'll find a tiny slip of a girl selling tickets or calling trains and out in the yards great husky Slavic women operating steam hammers.

You'll run across college-girl draftsmen, women lawyers and doctors, women telegraph operators and young kids at switchboards. You'll be surprised at the small women in tough jobs and big women in desk jobs.

You'll even find housewife drawbridge tenders and crossing flagmen.

They are all Americans, with as many races, creeds, and nationalities as there are jobs. And in this and every industry there are as many reasons for their taking those jobs as there are women.

Many have found fields opened to their talents for the first time. Many are there for the money or to follow the crowds.

Many Replace Their Own Men Who Are in the Service

Mainly, however, they are there because there *is* some man in service. They are working to supplement that slim G.I. envelope. And they are fighting to keep the country running, to keep the world supplied, to get their man the stuff he needs so he can get through and get back.

Like the steel which goes from women's hands in this country to the hands of women in the Soviet. It's one movement with one idea. The same steel for men moving from the West and men coming from the East. And women to help get it there.

It all works together. And as the war goes on, the great feel of it and the great interdependence of it gather strength. It's a man's and woman's world.

Discussion Questions

- The author uses language that is considered sexist today. Identify the sexist language in the essay and determine what impact you think that language had on readers in 1944.

- What is the author's tone in the article? Do you think the tone would be different if it were written by a male reporter?

- Why does the author include male co-workers' responses to the women? What point is she making with these responses?

- Why do you think the author often focuses on how the women are dressed? How does that relate to the main point of her essay?

Writing Activities

- Write an analytical essay on what happened to American working women at the end of World War II. How many were able to hold onto their jobs? How contented were those who went back to working exclusively in the home?

- Write an essay focusing on the impact World War II had on the women's movement in the United States.

- Write a personal essay about how you or someone close to you dealt with an incident of sexism.

Collaborative Activities

- The article notes that during World War II, "about a third of America's manpower ... [was] woman power." Divide into groups and interview women who worked during the war or their children about how they were able to handle the pressures of working outside of the home while taking care of a family. Report your findings to the class.

- The author notes the initial resistance to women working in jobs traditionally held by men, including welding and handling large cranes. Discuss in your group whether there are any jobs today that should be considered better suited to men. Be prepared to debate this issue with the class.

MOUNT ATHOS

In "Mount Athos," Merle Severy documents his trip to the monasteries of Mount Athos, a clifftop retreat on the northeastern edge of Greece. The article details the austere lives of the monks who have come to the monasteries for spiritual fulfillment.

As you read "Mount Athos," you should consider the following questions:

- Why did the monks come to Mount Athos?
- What are their lives like there?
- Why do you think women are not allowed?

Far away from the worries of the rest of humanity, the Simonopetra Monastery towers high above the Aegean Sea on a small peninsula of northeastern Greece. Founded in the mid-14th century, it stands like a fortress with 19 other Eastern Orthodox monasteries and a host of small compounds in a religious community named after snowcapped Mount Athos, background. Within these sanctuaries, pious men retreat from the world in a tradition dating back to the start of the Byzantine era.

MOUNT
ATHOS

Church walls are covered with frescoes, the earliest from the late 12th century. The monks' libraries hold about 15,000 manuscripts, many from the classical and medieval periods. Treasured relics include reputed fragments of the True Cross, a cloth dropped by the Virgin Mary at Calvary, and part of Christ's crown of thorns.

MONKS AT THE STAVRONIKETA MONASTERY
DO NOT PERMIT WOMEN
THE SAME PRIVILEGES AS THEY ENJOY. THAT HAS BEEN THEIR TRADITION FOR CENTURIES.

Saints ruled the lives of men who died in faith. A mosaic at Stavroniketa Monastery earned its name—St. Nicholas of the Oyster—in the 16th century after fishermen found the icon with an oyster embedded in its forehead.

At Simonopetra monks pile the bones of brothers in a charnel house. The remains of a former abbot rest in a special box held by Father Macarius. To the monks who pray here, these orderly rows of skulls evoke the monastery's long history and the devotion of the men who kept alive its spirit. The inscription on a skull—at St. Anne's monastic community—records the death of a Father Gregentios in 1979.

The monasteries are living museums of Byzantine culture.

Hermit monks came to Mount Athos as early as the ninth century. The first monastery, Great Lavra, was founded by St. Athanasios in 963 with financial help from the Byzantine emperor. By 1400, 19 of the 20 monasteries active today had been completed. Expansion later took place among the *sketes,* or outlying ascetic settlements. Some 1,500 monks now inhabit the Holy Mountain.

The monasteries are living museums of Byzantine culture.

Adapted from "Mount Athos" by Merle Severy: National Geographic Magazine, December 1983.

Now women may visit Mount Athos, under a constitution followed since 1045. But men with religious or scholarly purposes are welcome to free food and lodging. Meals are simple and solemn at the Stavroniketa Monastery, where the monks refresh themselves with soup, olives, bread, and wine, as one brother reads a lesson against gluttony. Most monasteries follow a Byzantine system of time that begins the day at sunset.

The majority of the monasteries are run as strict communes. The rest are less rigid, allowing monks to have personal property and to keep their own hours. No fish may be eaten during Lent. But at a branch of St. Paul's Monastery called New Skete, Father Spiridon believes that there should still be just a little for the cats.

© JAMES L. STANFIELD/National Geographic Image Collection

Discussion Questions

- Why do you think the author claims in the first sentence that the monks on Mount Athos are "far away from the worries of the rest of humanity"? How do you think this statement relates to the rest of the article?

- Why do you think the author does not provide many personal details about the monks?

- What effect does the picture of the skulls have on your response to the story? Why do you think the author included this picture?

- Why do you think the author does not explore in depth the reasons the monks came to Mount Athos? What questions would you like to ask them about why they are there?

Writing Activities

- Conduct research to determine whether or not women can be legally banned from any male club or association in the United States. Then write an argument for or against men banning women from organized groups.

- The author does not provide much detail about the monks' motivation for living such a secluded life. Find out about other men and women who have lived as spiritual hermits and write an essay analyzing the causes and effects of such a choice.

Collaborative Activities

- Find out whether women are still banned from Mount Athos. Decide as a group whether or not women should be banned from living among the monks. Be prepared to defend your response to the class.

- Discuss with your group what you think would motivate the monks to "retreat from the world."

- Watch the award-winning film *Of Gods and Men*, which focuses on a group of seven monks in an Algerian monastery. Write an analysis of the monastic life depicted in the film.

SICILY THE THREE-CORNERED

In "Sicily the Three-Cornered," Luis Marden chronicles his trip to Sicily, a mountainous island off the coast of Italy, where he observes men growing citrus, mining sulphur, and fishing the sea.

As you read "Sicily the Three-Cornered," you should consider the following questions:

- What are the men's various roles on the island?
- What are the rituals involved in fishing?
- What is the nature of the interaction between the author and the inhabitants?

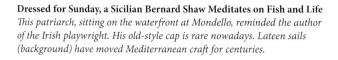

Dressed for Sunday, a Sicilian Bernard Shaw Meditates on Fish and Life
This patriarch, sitting on the waterfront at Mondello, reminded the author of the Irish playwright. His old-style cap is rare nowadays. Lateen sails (background) have moved Mediterranean craft for centuries.

SICILY THE THREE-CORNERED

Photographs by Luis Marden

Modern Vulcans, Grimacing in Heat and Smoke, Fit an Iron Tire to a Carved Wheel

Heated to a red glow, the tire is forced over the rim with levers, clamps, and hammers. Slight inequalities in the wood are burned away by the hot metal. As the tire cools, it shrinks and clamps itself to the wheel. These men work on the outskirts of Palermo, the center of wagon art. Most Sicilian wagons are drawn by horses, though some are hauled by mules. Donkey

ON THE MEDITERRANEAN'S BIGGEST ISLAND,
CRUCIBLE OF MANY CULTURES,
MEN GROW CITRUS, MINE SULPHUR, AND PATIENTLY FISH THE SEA

The Greeks had a word for it. They called it Trinacria, the three-cornered. Yet the Greeks, who colonized Sicily 700 years before Christ and remained for five centuries, were only one wave in a sea of peoples that has surged over the mountainous island.

The cultural heritage of Sicily is as many-layered as an onion. Peel away the Italian outer skin and you find the Normans; lift another layer and you see the Saracens; strip off another to disclose the Romans; under these lie the Carthaginians; then a stratum of Greeks; yet one more thickness reveals the Phoenicians; and so to the inner core of Sicans and Sicels, the shadowy early races.

Ancestry Shows in Sicilian Faces

One sees the faces of all these peoples in the crowds that throng the streets of Palermo, the capital. This handsome city facing the blue Tyrrhenian lies cupped in a mountain-girt plain, the Golden Shell. In the evening, crowds saunter along the capital's broad avenues and fill the cafes along the Via Ruggero Settimo. Customers crowd four deep at cafe counters.

Then after a lengthy wait, inky cafe espresso drips in a feeble trickle, a ludicrous contrast to the ritual of preparation.

A cashier enthroned in a booth sells tickets to the standing customers, who exchange them for coffee, elaborate pastries, or bitter vermouth-base apéritifs.

Here, in the land of their invention, I saw the Italian coffee-making machines in all their chrome-plated glory. The gleaming instruments incorporate shining cylindrical urns hung about with water gauges, ebony-handled spigots, valves, and yards of tubing. White-coated operators clamp a metal cup under a faucet, then spin wheels and pull levers while steam hisses and agitated water leaps up and down in a glass tube. Then, after a lengthy wait, inky *caffè espresso* drips in a feeble trickle, a ludicrous contrast to the ritual of preparation.

Coffee of Many Colors

But what wonderful coffee! Strong, black, and fragrant, it is served in tiny cups half the size of a demitasse. There is a whole series of gradations

---

Adapted from "Sicily the Three-Cornered" by Luis Marden: National Geographic Magazine, January 1955.

in cafe coffee, from black to white. If you want a cup that is extremely strong, ask for a *restricted coffee;* for some less strong, say a *long coffee;* if you prefer coffee with a little milk, ask for a *Capuchin,* which is probably named for the color of the monks' habit.

Many of Sicily's regional dishes come from the sea, for, above all, Sicilians are fishermen. From ancient times they have followed the old and honorable calling, and Sicily has sent her sons to man the fishing fleets of many nations. In the United States there are colonies of Sicilian fishermen in Boston, Gloucester, San Francisco, and other ports.

I liked to wander about in this city of imposing baroque buildings in search of interesting little *trattorie,* humbler and more typical eating places than the full-fledged restaurants. Down in the narrow streets near Palermo's waterfront one can eat a wonderful dish of spaghetti with squid sauce, or plates of red mullet or fried octopus. The red mullet were prized by the Romans; even today I found them to be expensive and scarce.

Squid and octopus swarm in Sicilian waters. Without these soft, big-eyed cephalopods Italian cookery would lose many savory dishes.

I went squid fishing one night with a man named Filippo. He kept his rowboat in a small basin protected by a breakwater and a disused lighthouse. The flame of an acetylene lamp hissed steadily and lighted Filippo's wise-monkey face as he rowed us into the darkness. With sly winks he told me of an unusual red-spotted squid he had caught.

"I took it to the scientifics at the museum," he said, "and they beat the pages of their big books looking for it, but they couldn't tell me what it was. It tasted good, though."

As we rowed over the oily black water, yellow lights like stars winked on and off. They were the little flames of other squid fishermen. As the boats rose and fell with the slow swell, the rising shoulder of the sea occulted the lights; then the black waters slid away and the yellow points blinked on again.

There are more Sicilians in Brooklyn than in Palermo.

Squid Strike at Baitless Hooks

I could see nothing but the lights and a few pale stars when Filippo suddenly cried, *"Viva Maria!"* From the blackness a voice replied, *"Viva Gesù!"*

We pulled alongside another fisherman whose bent back had concealed his light from us. When Filippo asked, "What luck?" the man, piety forgotten, burst out with, "Ah, pig of a goddess, there are no blanked inhabitants in this blanked piece of sea!"

Squid are caught on an artificial lure that looks like a miniature mushroom anchor, armed with a circlet of needle-pointed barb-less hooks. The squid strike at the lure as it is seesawed up and down about 50 feet below the boat. Our friend who was working the empty piece of sea fished two lines; one was tied to his ear and the other he jigged up and down in one hand.

The fisherman suddenly began to pull in his line, swiftly but smoothly, hand over hand, until at last with a heave he swung the lure with its clinging squid into the boat. As he jerked the catch out of the water, my exploding camera flash caught the string of water globules in mid-air; for an instant they hung, frozen in an arc, motionless and glistening like bubbles of crystal in suspension.

When we rowed back to Palermo, cold, tired, and hungry, about 3 o'clock in the morning, we had only a few small squid in the boat.

Sicilian Roads Climb and Plunge

There are few straight and level stretches of road in Sicily. From Palermo I drove westward along the coast road, behind the jutting headland of Mount Pellegrino, and through the little town of Sferracavallo, with its blocks of old buildings huddled in the shadow of a fantastically shaped rock. The yellow sunlight lay like butter on the stone buttress above the town, and, a little distance beyond, the setting sun drew red streaks along the horizon, silhouetting the stone tower on a small island offshore.

Trapani, an old city of narrow crowded streets on a long peninsula that points its finger at the Egadi Islands offshore, panted in a pall of heat. My host at the hotel said, "If you want to cool off, go up there," and pointed to an isolated mountain that loomed in the moonlight beyond the city.

Rising 2,400 feet above Trapani's shimmering heat, one of Sicily's most fascinating towns stands on this lonely mountain. Erice, the ancient Eryx, has no exact founding date. Even in classical times its origins were lost in the dimness of antiquity and had assumed the status of a myth. At that time it was the center of a cult of Venus, here considered the protecting goddess of seafarers.

When I drove through a gate in Erice's thick wall, I left behind the world of clangorous cities. All was silence; cold winds whistled down deserted cobblestone streets. Barred and shuttered houses everywhere seemed not so much hostile as reserved and peaceful.

Uncle Vito Offers Help

One castle has been restored and is used as a villa, a place of retirement from summer heat. It stands on the brink of nothing. Below it the thick mist swirled and blotted out the view of the coast below.

As I stood at the rail of a little park waiting for the mist to clear, an old man wearing a hooded cloak approached, announced that he was more than 80 years old, that his name was Uncle Vito, and that he would answer any questions about Erice.

The break in the fog came with surprising suddenness. At my feet I saw the headland of Trapani stretching into the hazy sea. Evaporating basins for sea salt surrounded the port with a geometric pattern.

Along the steep streets of Erice walk silent black-mantled women. Uncle Vito hailed one and introduced me. Her name was Aunt Bartola and she was 86, but, like Vito, spry, upright, and full of good humor. She accompanied us nimbly round the city wall, pointing out ogival church doorways and an occasional Norman inscription. Back in the little central piazza, I offered her a ride in my car.

"This is the second time in my life that I have been in a motorcar," she said. "The last time was in 1916."

She held tightly to her black silk mantle as we drove round outside the walls on the edge of the plateau. When we reached the giddy speed of 35 miles an hour, I heard her mutter under her breath, "Blessed devil, how did you come to mix me up in this situation?"

Like nearly all Sicilians, Aunt Bartola had relatives in America. "Perhaps you know my nephew in Brooklyn?" she asked. "Yes," added Uncle Vito, voicing a mistaken belief of many islanders, "there are more Sicilians in Brooklyn than in Palermo."

Big Families the Rule on Sicily

Overpopulation—families of 14 and 15 children are not uncommon among country people—and absentee ownership of large estates, with little arable land to go round among ordinary people, are largely responsible for the great outflow of migrants from what is, after all, an agriculturally rich island.

Uncle Vito led me along the railed walk that runs so close to the edge of the plateau that one seems to stand on the flying bridge of a ship. With the heavy white mist hiding everything below I had a sensation of weightlessness, of being suspended in space and time.

"And that," said Uncle Vito, "is the Temple of Venus."

I was a bit disappointed. The "temple" is a crumbling medieval ruin clinging to the edge of an outthrust spur that drops sheer to the rocky lower slopes.

Uncle Vito described how in classical times the handsomest girls gathered round the temple to do homage to the goddess by sacrificing themselves to returning mariners in their own fashion. The old boy nodded.

"Belli tempi, quelli!" he said. (Fascinating times, those!)

Sicily's Most Famous View

Halfway between Catania and Messina stands the town with the most famous view in Sicily. Taormina is so squeezed on its lofty natural terrace that everything there seems miniature—the extremely narrow streets, the tiny squares, the minuscule cafes. But the world drops away at the edge of the mountain, and one can sit sipping coffee and look southward across Sicily—almost, it seems, to Africa.

Northward I drove to Messina, the city closest to the Italian mainland, a scant five miles from the peninsula of Italy. Ever since the terrible earthquake of 1908, in which 60,000 died and more than 90 percent of the city's buildings were razed, Messina has erected only low structures of reinforced concrete along its wide streets and avenues. It has the most modern look of Sicily's cities

I wanted to see the peculiar form of swordfishing practiced in the Strait of Messina, so I drove northward along the beach, passing through towns with wonderful names like Paradise and Peace to Ganzirri.

From April through August the black-hulled swordfishing boats are strung like sentinels along the shores of Messina. They anchor close to shore at 20 stations, which are allocated by the Captain of the Port at the beginning of each season. The stations have such names as Prince, Fountain, Breast, Beautiful, Dirty, Saint Agatha, and Grotto, and are rotated among the fleet.

On the station a big boat, the *feluca*, with a disproportionately tall mast, serves as a floating observation platform. Two small craft, the *ontri*, tie up to the parent vessel. Atop the high mast a lookout stands for a 4-hour trick, scanning through narrowed eyelids the blue sunlit strait.

The lookout usually faces upstream, as fish swimming with the current are swept by rapidly; occasionally he turns and searches the sea around him.

Current Reverses Every Six Hours

"Downstream" and "upstream" are not fixed terms in the strait, because the 6-mile-an-hour current normally changes direction

But it was typical of the generosity of the Sicilian fisherman that they immediately invited me to join them.

every six hours. The Ionian Sea to the south and the Tyrrhenian at the north end of the narrow strait have different tidal levels, and, when the tide changes, this difference causes violent currents and whirlpools.

I sat in one of the small boats several hours a day for three days, waiting for the appearance of a fish.

Six men man these little craft: the boss, who is also the harpooner; four oarsmen; and the lookout, who directs the actual pursuit of a swordfish. I was eager to film this mode of fishing, but I had been told that it would be impossible for me to get into the small boat that did the harpooning because I would be in the way during the speed and excitement of the chase. But it was typical of the generosity of the Sicilian fishermen that they immediately invited me to join them. While we sat in the rocking boat under the blazing sun, the men tossed me bits of swordfishing lore.

Classical sailors dreaded the passage through the strait, particularly through the narrow part close to where we were anchored. Here a rock called Scylla on the Italian mainland nearly touches the point of Sicily, three-and-a-half miles away. Off the Sicilian shore the ancients placed Charybdis, a monster lying in wait for luckless mariners. Actually it is a whirlpool. They also feared a monster that lived in a cave in the rock of Scylla.

The hours dragged on, the lookout clung to his high platform, and some of the men fell asleep.

We had been three days without sighting a fish, though our position moved up one station each day. The men, whose daily bread—literally—depended on their success, talked ruefully, but without real bitterness.

To while away the time, Nino, one of the crew, stood up and began to sing in a Sicilian imitation of the Neapolitan dialect.

A shout from the lookout came with such suddenness that Nino tumbled into the stern sheets as the captain leaped for the painter and cast off. Everyone automatically took his place, the men at the oars standing facing forward, the captain on his harpooner's platform forward, and Nino on his short lookout mast amidships.

I jumped on the midships thwart, my left arm and leg round the stubby mast, my right leg spread wide with the foot close to the gunwale, so that the oarsman immediately behind me could sweep forward without striking me with the loom of his oar.

Harpooning a Swordfish

Hugging the mast with my left arm and with Nino's feet just touching my head, I held the camera to my eye. As eager as I was to make the picture, my chief fear was of hindering my kind friends in the capture of their first fish in three days.

All this had taken about five seconds. Now we were scudding over the water, guided by the shouted directions of the lookout high above the big vessel. The swordfish first circled out to sea, then doubled on his track.

When Nino caught sight of him, he jumped up and down in frenzied eagerness, the soles of his feet slapping my head as he shouted, *"Forte, Nicolo! Forte, Francesco!"*

The fish straightened and swam just beneath the surface as we closed to five yards, when suddenly the lookout cried, "Stop all!" Silent now, the boat shot a length ahead, pushing a suddenly audible bow wave, and at the same instant the boss cried, "Blessed St. Mark!" and let fly his 14-foot harpoon. It struck solidly, the line snaked out from the basket where it lay in coils, and the swordfish, held fast by the barbed spearhead, towed the boat out to sea.

The fishermen calculate half an hour to each 100 pounds when bringing a fish to boat. This time ours came in quickly, as he weighed only 90 pounds. Small as he was, the men were overjoyed at catching something after so long a wait. With a formal air the captain cut out the choice saddle just back of the shoulder and presented it to me. I protested, but the crew would not hear of my not accepting.

My good friends put me ashore at Ganzirri beach, pointing out a restaurant where, they said, the swordfish would be cooked in proper Messina style.

An hour later I sat on the terrace, facing the strait, which at the change of tides, the "balanced waters" of the fishermen, reflected a mauve afterglow on its glassy surface. I had eaten a couple of dozen fresh mussels, which had been cultivated in the lagoon at my back. Now my host placed his masterpiece before me: roast swordfish steak, with pungent Sicilian lemon and a delicate caper sauce. A dry and heady white wine from the slopes of Etna completed one of the repasts that I shall always remember, both for itself and for the generosity of the humble men who furnished its centerpiece.

Wind and Fire Gods Dwelt on Vulcano

One day I sailed from Messina through the strait to the Aeolian Islands (Isole Eolie). We nosed out of the harbor at dawn, over leadenly glistening water, past the cape of Scylla, and out into the suddenly blue Tyrrhenian Sea.

Italians are a nation of divers. From earliest times the inhabitants of the peninsula and its islands have gone down into their limpid seas. Frogmen and goggle fishermen first saw bottom here. During the days of the Empire the Romans employed men with the curious Latin name of *urinatores*—divers—to swim just under the surface, breathing from goatskins or through reed tubes, and approach enemy ships to scuttle them or set them afire.

And the modern sport of underwater hunting of fish first became formalized in Italy. Today there are no more enthusiastic gogglers than the Italians, and history records what the frogmen, riding astride 2-man torpedoes of Italian invention, did to the British naval units in Gibraltar and Alexandria.

Never have I seen seas so clear as in the Volcanic Islands. When I floated in the waters off Vulcano and Stromboli, *(Continued on page 104)*

Donkey's reward: a taste of sulla from his own burden. The animal's owner greeted the author in Italian mixed with Greek, Spanish, and French, a dialect reflecting the passage of Sicily's many conquerors. Italy's official and literary speech is the Tuscan of the north. Sicily's country dialects bear little resemblance to the tongue of Dante.

(Continued from page 101) I seemed to be suspended over a soundless landscape that suggested the dead vistas of the moon.

At Strombolicchio—Little Stromboli—I watched goggle fishermen jackknife, then surface dive vertically downward, swimming with the aid of rubber fins. Staying under for more than a minute, they peered into crevices in the face of the rock looking for the *cernia*, a fat grouper. I saw one goggler thrust his gun into a crack, heard a dull *chung*, and watched the fisherman haul in a struggling 15-pound fish.

Italians, though they pioneered in the use of oxygen-breathing apparatus, are especially adept at diving without breathing equipment. In 1952 Lt. Raimondo Bucher of the Italian Air Force achieved the world's record depth. Wearing only a goggle and rubber fins, he dived to an amazing 128 feet off Capri.

Stromboli is nothing more than a volcanic cone rising from the sea. There is barely room for the island's little towns to cling to the edges of the mountain, which rises from a 3,000-foot depth.

Tuna Trap Brought by Moors

One day in Palermo I received a telegram from the director of the Favignana fishery: The tuna had appeared in force and it was time for a *mattanza*—a killing.

I took ship at Trapani to go over to the Egadi Islands to see the great *tonnara* of Favignana, largest in the Mediterranean. The tonnara is the system of nets stretched across the migration path of the giant fish.

There are stone quarries on Favignana, and the people grow some grapes, but tuna fishing is the chief business of the island. In a wineshop that night the secretary of the fishery introduced me to some of the fishermen who would man the nets at dawn next morning.

I met the *rais*, captain of the fishery, a mustached old man with kindly eyes and a sharp jutting chin. The Arabic word "rais" is one of many Moorish terms used in the tonnara. The rais told me that the tonnara had been brought to Sicily from North Africa and that the records of the Favignana nets went back unbroken to the 17th century.

"We have a man constantly on watch," said the rais. "He looks down through a glass-bottomed bucket and counts the fish as they come in. Then he opens the netting doors to let the fish pass from one chamber to another. When he thinks there are enough to warrant a killing, he sends word to me."

At dawn I stood on the pier beneath a high bare hill and watched the black boats assemble in the yellow morning light. The heavy work boats were towed out in a long string to the nets about a mile offshore. I went in the last small boat with the rais.

The tonnara is a net system stretching from the surface to the ocean floor in two main parts. The foot, a barrier a mile and a half long, stretches from the shore across the migration path of the tuna. This net deflects the fish, which turn shoreward and then encounter another, shorter barrier that conducts them to the door leading into a series of enclosed traps or chambers. The last of these, the "chamber of death," is the only one that has a netting floor. When the tuna are at last gathered in this trap, the men haul the floor almost to the surface, then pull out the wildly charging fish with hooks on the ends of long poles. This is the mattanza.

Our towboat cast us off close to a bobbing buoy. The men took off their caps and chorused, "Good morning, St. Peter!" The saint's picture on the buoy seemed to nod.

Fish Swim into Chamber of Death

The other boats continued on to the lines of floats marking the end of the series of chambers and formed a U round three sides of the chamber of death.

Our little boat moved in over the gate and down to the second of the eight chambers. The boat had a small glass-bottomed well amidships, and I sat over this, huddled under an old sail. I pressed my face to the luminous blue-green window, and when my eyes grew accustomed to the dim light, I saw them. Enormous shadowy fish, fusiform and compact as submarines, slowly swimming about 20 feet down, endlessly going round in counterclockwise circles. Their sickle tails flicked from side to side, and flecks of yellow light gleamed from caudal finlets.

As I watched, a head and a powerful whiff of tobacco entered my sail tent.

"Pretty, eh?" said the head. "That big one'll go better than 700 pounds. Why don't they break out? Ha, they could if they tried; the netting's only thin coconut fiber! But—" the fisherman chuckled—"right now the tuna are foolish, because they are in love. It doesn't occur to a lovesick tuna to try to break out of a net; no, he swims patiently round and round, like a sheep."

The sea is 100 feet deep at this point, and the tuna would sometimes sink so deep as they circled that they became ghostly yellow-green outlines in the cobalt depths.

Another boat had moved up to the entrance to the next chamber. With a boat hook a man lifted the netting door.

Broken Crockery Lures Tuna

A fisherman at the open gate threw bits of broken white crockery in the water. As they sank, the shards fluttered like falling leaves, and their surfaces sent moons of white light glancing through the water. Eventually a curious tuna would go to investigate, then swim through the gate.

When the great fish came close to my window, I could see marks of bites they had given each other, the fishermen said, in amorous excitement. Suddenly I saw them stream toward the gate, head to tail, in one swift movement. Like sheep, they had all followed the leader. The netting was pulled up behind them, and we settled to wait patiently for them to move into the next chamber and then, finally, into the fatal last chamber.

Right now the tuna are foolish, because they are in love.

When they were all in and the gate had been closed, the black *vascello*, biggest boat of all, moved in. Only the rais's boat remained inside the closed rectangle.

The net on three sides of the rectangle had already been hauled to take up slack from the "body," or net floor. Now the vascello men, standing on broad gunwales, began to pull the flooring up from its 100-foot depth.

They pulled anyhow at first; then, as the heaviest netting neared the top, they began a chantey, swaying and hauling in unison like a corps de ballet. They chanted in Sicilian mixed with Arabic:

E' San Petru piscaturi
Aia mola! Aia mola!

The rectangle of sea, sheltered by the black hulls and the crowded fishermen, remained green and calm at first. As the net floor came closer to the surface, black shapes darted about in panic, tail fins cut the water, and a shout rose from the men. Then pandemonium broke loose.

The beating tails of charging fish sent fountains of spray into the air, and the water boiled as they hurled themselves at the netting walls. But this part of the net was made of heavy rope, and their effort was useless. The fish churned madly as the men fastened off the net and picked up hooked poles. With shouts and imprecations they stabbed at the mass of churning fish, two or three hooking into the same torpedo body.

As many as six men would take hold of one 600-pound tuna to pull the monster over the gunwale. There would come a point when the water no longer buoyed up the great weight and the giant fish was poised halfway, when the group seemed frozen as in a tableau. Suddenly the men would give one more concerted heave, and the fish would tip and slide headfirst into the boat as the men bent like sheaves of wheat on each side, away from the thrashing tail that was capable of crushing a skull with one blow.

As the heavy vascello filled with the thrashing fish, it trembled with the vibration of the monsters. The sea reddened with blood. Spray spouted into the air, and the men, maddened by the primitive struggle, yelled, shouted, and cursed.

One by one the fish came into the boat and the tumult died down, until a small lone tuna, which had been ceaselessly circling his prison, was harpooned and boated.

Fishermen Give Thanks for Catch

Then, as suddenly as the uproar had begun, there fell a dead silence. The fishermen, standing on the gunwales in their wet and bloodstained clothes, removed their caps and bowed their heads, thanking God for sending them once more the harvest of the sea.

The net floor was unfastened and allowed to sink slowly to the bottom; the boats formed once more in line and were taken in tow. I rode in the vascello with the 88 tuna. The sea was strangely quiet and peaceful after the noise and excitement of the last half hour.

As we came into harbor, three fishing vessels hoisted rust-red sails and moved slowly out to sea to take up their positions for the night's work. The cycle of fishing, like that of life itself, goes endlessly on in Sicily.

Discussion Questions

- What do you think the author's attitude is toward the men on the island? How is this attitude expressed?

- Why does the author spend so much time detailing the tasks involved in fishing? How do these details give us a fuller portrait of Sicilian men?

- Why do you think the author includes details of his time with Uncle Vito? Is he an effective illustration of any points about Sicily that the author makes?

- Explain the effect of the inclusion of the author's experiences on the fishing boat. Why didn't he limit his focus to the fishermen?

- How does the article end? How effective is this conclusion?

Writing Activities

- Watch the film *The Perfect Storm* about a group of men fishing off of the New England coast and write an analytical essay that focuses on how the fishermen are depicted.

- Investigate places where the fishing industry has had a negative impact on the environment. Then write an argument for or against restrictions on fishing in these areas.

Collaborative Activities

- In groups of two, conduct research on how the people of Sicily make their living today. Determine whether the men and women still have traditional roles or whether those traditions have been broken.

- From groups and name stories and films that focus on fishermen. What do they have in common? Why do you think stories about fishermen are popular?

THE MAKING OF
AN ASTRONAUT

Robert R. Gilruth writes about how astronauts prepared for the Project Gemini space mission in 1965 and the orbital and lunar voyages that followed it. Gilruth documents the grueling physical conditioning, as well as the long hours of lectures and technical meetings that made up their regimen.

As you read "The Making of an Astronaut," you should consider the following questions:

- What did the astronauts have to learn about the spacecraft they would fly?
- How did they condition their bodies to withstand the stresses that they would encounter in space?
- How has flight simulation become an important part of the training?

Gemini simulator trains flight and ground personnel in all phases of an actual mission except docking. Astronaut Mike Collins (foreground) and NASA engineer John Sargent share the controls. Hal Parker of Flight Crew Support Division watches through a hatch that would close in flight. Technicians monitor the mission at the control console in background.

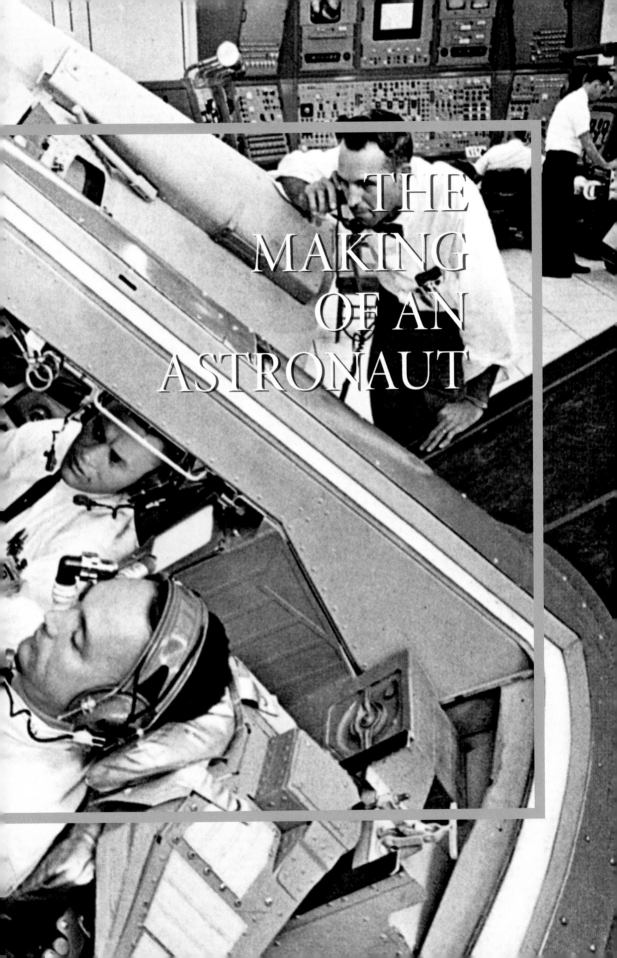

THE MAKING OF AN ASTRONAUT

Wet touchdown, simulated in Galveston Bay, Texas: *a Gemini team practicing egress from spacecraft. NASA divers stand by in a rubber life raft. Gemini and Apollo space teams coming back from lunar flights hope to drop into the shock-absorbing sea, as Mercury astronauts did.*

BECOMING AN ASTRONAUT WAS
AND HAS BEEN

AN INTENSE AND DEMANDING PROCESS.

ALTHOUGH THERE ARE NOW WOMEN ASTRONAUTS,
IN THE 1960S, ONLY MEN WERE CONSIDERED FOR IT.

This is The Year of Gemini.

Before 1965 is many months old, a powerful Titan II rocket will blast off from Cape Kennedy, carrying two American astronauts aboard a spacecraft called Gemini—after the twins of the zodiac. For more than two years these men and their fellow astronauts have prepared themselves for Project Gemini and the epochal lunar voyages that will follow. They have pursued a unique training curriculum, and their classrooms lie scattered throughout the country.

They have attended hundreds of lectures, pored over thousands of documents, and sat through countless technical meetings.

They have conditioned their bodies to withstand grueling combinations of stresses: acceleration, weightlessness, noise, heat, cold, vibration, disorientation, and immobilization.

They have learned to survive in Panama's tropical jungles and in Nevada's scorching deserts. They have studied the geology of steaming fumaroles, lava tubes, and ice caves. They have sunk their pickaxes into basalt, shale, and pre-Cambrian rocks.

They have visited factories to watch embryo spacecraft take shape. They have practiced

Such exacting preparations have made American astronauts the world's most active commuters.

with dozens of training devices, simulating possible accidents and how to avoid them.

Such exacting preparations have made American astronauts the world's most active commuters. Flying sleek, white-bellied supersonic trainers, they race the sun from coast to coast, squeezing extra hours out of the day and dragging white contrails in a crazy-quilt pattern across the heavens from Florida to California, Long Island to Oregon, St. Louis to the Nation's Capital.

And, finally, home.

Home is the National Aeronautics and Space Administration's Manned Spacecraft Center near Houston, Texas, 1,620 acres of laboratories, test chambers, and offices. Across its geometrical landscape, the great adventure of our time unfolds: a trip to the moon.

To understand the magnitude of these events, look at the recent history of space. Less than two years ago, I stood in the Mercury Control Center as Maj. L. Gordon Cooper, Jr., hurtled into orbit in his 4,000-pound, one-man capsule on this nation's longest space flight: 34⅓ hours.

Adapted from "The Making of an Astronaut" by Robert R. Gilruth: National Geographic Magazine, January 1965.

Now the 7,000-pound Gemini awaits her two-man crew and much longer orbital journeys.

Rendezvous in Space Comes First

Gemini flights are an intermediate step in our moon-flight program. They will permit us to study the effects of weightlessness for up to two weeks and teach us the technology required to bring two vehicles together in space. We must master space rendezvous if we are to reach for the moon later. In our Gemini program, managed by Charles W. Mathews, astronauts will practice this complex maneuver with the unmanned Agena vehicle, separately launched on an Atlas missile.

Before the end of this decade, the 34-story Apollo-Saturn V vehicle will carry men to the moon. Apollo consists of two spacecraft: the 57,000-pound Command and Service Modules in which three men will travel to and from the moon, and the 29,000-pound Lunar Excursion Module (LEM) in which two of the crew will land on the lunar surface while the third orbits the moon in the Command Module, awaiting their return.

If the Mercury vehicle is the Wright *Flyer* of the Space Age, certainly the Apollo ranks as the jet transport of space flight. Moreover, space progress is accelerating. More than half a century passed between the Wright *Flyer* and commercial jets. Less than a decade will separate earth-girdling Mercury from the lunar touchdown of Apollo. And who knows what lies beyond?

As Director of the NASA Manned Spacecraft Center, I have watched the growth of our nation's space technology. I remember the makeshift quarters in which a few of us gathered in 1958 to begin Project Mercury. Today, from my ninth-story window in our Project Management Building, I look out on some of the world's finest specialized facilities for manned space flight, now rapidly approaching completion.

For example, the nine-story building to my left contains a 120-foot-high chamber in which a full-size spacecraft and its crew will experience a simulation of the moon's hostile environment. Chamber walls filled with liquid nitrogen expose Apollo's skin to the −280° F. of the nighttime

lunar surface. Through portholes on one side and above, racks of glaring searchlights bake the craft at 260° F., the daytime maximum.

Our earliest lunar explorers probably will not have to endure such extremes of temperature when walking about the moon's surface; they may land in an area not illuminated by direct sunlight but by earthshine, the reflected light of our own planet. But their space suits must be designed—and successfully tested—to withstand any eventuality. Without the bulky protective suit, a trip into the chamber would be like having one foot in the deep freeze and the other in the barbecue pit.

We expect to take care of the heat and cold with insulation and a small backpack containing a life-support system. But the suit, when pressurized in a vacuum, becomes stiff and hinders movement. The astronauts will need practice working with it under realistic conditions.

They can get much of their training right here at our Manned Spacecraft Center. With more than 20 buildings—ultimately there will be some 60—the center resembles a modern university. Its office buildings surround a quadrangle dotted with live oaks, pines, and pools. Here we see a major segment of accumulated scientific knowledge at work, attacking the unbelievably difficult problems of sustaining man in space.

Like a university, this campus has a faculty: 2,200 of this country's most experienced aerospace engineers and scientists, supported by nearly 2,200 technicians, administrators, and clerical workers. Besides managing development of spacecraft, our people pursue advanced research projects; they also spend much time in the classroom, both teaching and being taught.

But our best-known students are the astronauts. Their training is the most intensive and expensive. They spend 50 hours a week for two to five years training for a single flight. On lunar missions, each crew will be responsible for a vehicle costing more than the entire training program for all the astronauts.

We provide only postgraduate training for the astronauts. Their preparation really began years ago in college, where most of them obtained engineering or science degrees. Then came flight training and as many as ten years as jet pilots. Many have had a graduate course in test-pilot school.

Experienced pilots, they have excellent health, emotional stability, and coolness under pressure. They have operated aircraft under the most dangerous conditions; nine have flown in combat. They have faced fear and learned to overcome it.

Our astronaut team now totals 28 members, including six of our original seven-man Mercury team, nine "intermediate" class members brought aboard for the two-man Gemini flights, and 13 of an original 14 "freshmen" just completing their first full year of space training. Later this year we will select a dozen or so additional astronauts with emphasis on their science background.

Studies Include Comets and Computers

Our Astronaut Training Program covers four major areas:

The Spacecraft: Each man must become thoroughly familiar with all the space vehicles, how they are built, and how they fly.

The Space Environment: Each must learn to feel at home in the weightlessness of space; the weak lunar gravity, only one-sixth that of earth; forbidding temperature extremes, and the crushing forces of launch and re-entry.

Space Survival: Each must learn how to eject himself from his spacecraft should something go wrong during launch or re-entry, and to survive wherever he lands, in the water, desert, or jungle, until rescued.

Space Science: Each must become a skilled observer, with a knowledge of geology and astronomy, in order to bring back scientific information—a primary NASA goal.

In 200 hours of lectures, an astronaut learns about hypergolic fuels and hyperbolic velocities, about telemetry and temperature control, about everything from comets and cryogenics to computers and communications.

But astronauts need more than books and lectures. Spacecraft change as new systems are

We must **master space rendezvous if we are to reach for the moon later.**

added, old systems modified. Astronauts face the problem that troubled an old Swedish friend, who said: "I have hardly learned to say yob, and already they are calling it proyect."

The complexity of the program is such that one of the best ways to keep up to date is to work right with the engineers who design the spacecraft. This is one of the advantages of having the astronauts train at our center side by side with the skilled scientists who manage our spacecraft programs. By sitting in on engineering design meetings, the astronauts hear of modifications as soon as they are initiated.

One man cannot hope to attend all engineering sessions; each of the astronauts takes on a specialty and keeps the other 27 abreast of developments.

As spacecraft systems become more complex, we must use more elaborate training aids. Gemini, for example, uses "systems trainers"—billboard-size diagrams with special lighting effects to show the astronaut what lies behind the blinking signals and trembling needles of his instrument panel. When he throws switches on a mock panel, relays chatter, indicators flash, and routes light up in various patterns of color to show the flow of oxygen, water, and power through the systems. These devices unwind the intricate wiring of all the black boxes and lay it out in a map that the eye can follow and the mind understand.

So the astronauts acquire a basic understanding of their spacecraft. But that is quite different from actually operating the controls in split seconds and reacting instantly and accurately to emergencies. An airplane pilot can practice in the air with an instructor to take over in case of trouble. But in a spacecraft the astronaut is on his own from the first moment of flight. How to practice, then? With mechanical flight simulators.

The idea of simulation is not new. The Romans, faced with Carthaginian ea forces, had to learn techniques of naval warfare. They set up several galley frames on shore, and in these "fixed-base simulators" they trained crews to row and legionaries to board for hand-to-hand combat.

In contrast, space-flight simulation has become so complex that we can take it only in steps. At first the astronaut practices bits and pieces of the total mission in "part-task trainers."

We have converted the old Mercury procedures trainer into a part-task trainer for Gemini. In it the astronaut can practice one of the most difficult parts of the Gemini mission, seeking out and hooking up with the Agena spacecraft.

Out the window of this part-task trainer, the astronaut sees a dark void dusted with stars. As he maneuvers his simulated spacecraft, a blinking light glows brighter and brighter until it finally approaches close enough to reveal the cylindrical shape of the Agena vehicle.

To practice the complete two-man Gemini orbital mission requires a far more complex trainer than that used in Mercury. For this purpose we have had to build a new Gemini Full-Mission Simulator. Whenever I inspect this trainer I am always impressed by the roomful of computer equipment necessary to reproduce intricate Gemini maneuvers. Compared to the spinet-size Mercury trainer control console, Gemini's looks like a pipe organ.

Earth Floats Outside Trainer Window

Inside, the spacecraft reminds me of a sports car, with a control panel between the seats. Instead of ashtrays and glove compartments, this center console is studded with switches and knobs. From it projects the gearshiftlike control stick. Since both astronauts must be able to fly, the man sitting in the right-hand seat will have to use his left hand.

Squeezing down into the seat and pulling the hatch closed over your head, you find yourself crowded into a space slightly smaller than a phone booth. For an astronaut, this will be "home" for up to two weeks.

Its window is attached to a complex optical and color TV system which reproduces the view

For an astronaut this will be "home" for up to two weeks.

of the earth. From a hundred miles up, you see pinpoint stars in a black sky, and sunlit blue-green earth stretching almost 900 miles to the curving horizon.

Gemini is a highly maneuverable vehicle. Whereas Mercury, like a cannon ball, was limited to one trajectory or orbit, Gemini can change orbits and maneuver during re-entry to select the best landing point. The instrument panel reflects this complexity. Like a modern jet, it bristles with instruments showing the vehicle's attitude, position, engine status, and fuel supplies. Needles move and lights flicker on and off realistically as the instructor puts the trainer through its paces.

"4, 3, 2, 1, 0, lift-off."

With a simulated roar of Titan II rocket engines, your imaginary flight begins.

The spacecraft clock is running, and now the altimeter needle comes off the peg as the Titan rumbles its way skyward.

Then, seconds after lift-off, the black-and-white eight-ball altitude instrument rolls slightly to the left and then downward as the rocket arcs over and heads down range from Cape Kennedy.

"Two minutes, thirty seconds. Stand by for BECO."

A yellow light flashes on, indicating booster-engine cutoff. In a moment, a green light and a roar confirm that the Titan's second-stage engine has come to life.

"Five minutes, thirty seconds, guidance looks green. Stand by for SECO."

The read-out display of Gemini's timer slowly counts the seconds to the point of sustainer-engine cutoff. Now the engine roar gives way to silence, and you are in orbit, circling the earth at a speed of some 17,500 miles an hour.

I remember that Maj. Virgil I. Grissom was once asked what part of the Gemini flight would be the most difficult. "I guess the part between lift-off and landing," Gus replied.

LEM Pilot Must Land Carefully

Though the Gemini trainer seems complex, the Apollo simulator will surpass it. Stanley

Faber, chief of flight simulation, likes to tell visitors, "It will have everything, including—literally—a bathroom and a kitchen sink."

More than twice as large as the Gemini trainer, the Apollo equipment will actually consist of two units: the simulators of the Command Module and the LEM.

Among the many impressive features, an out-the-window display gives the crew a panoramic, make-believe journey through half a million miles of space. Nine tons of optical equipment produce this celestial extravaganza so accurately that astronauts can practice their critical star navigation and moon landings.

Though the Apollo simulators are not yet operational, we can get a good feel for what the moon landing in the LEM will be like in our Guidance and Control Division. Stepping through a doorway, one enters a cabin somewhat like the bridge of a ship. Instead of a ship's wheel, we find switches that can begin a make-believe landing.

Through a triangular window on the left glares a nightmare surface—red and yellow crosses and arrows grouped in squares like a patchwork quilt. This particular device cannot simulate the valleys and plains of the moon, as the actual LEM simulator will do, so it creates a completely abstract surface in full color.

Docking Trainer Rides Cushion of Air

Test pilot James Brickle describes the landing problem: "The autopilot starts you curving toward the lunar surface. You take over at 200 feet, as the LEM rushes downward. Your job is to slow it with your descent engine enough for a soft landing in a safe place—and you have only two minutes to do it. After that your landing fuel burns out. Without power, and with no air or parachute to slow you down, you would smash into the lunar surface."

But these stationary simulators have one thing in common: If you make a mistake, you do not smash into anything. You merely press the button marked "Reset" and start over.

For critical piloting tasks, we use simulators that move like the spacecraft themselves. One of these "moving-base" trainers, the Translation and Docking Simulator, is here at the center. It occupies a gymnasium-size building painted black inside to suggest the darkness of space.

Now, with Comdr. Walter M. Schirra, Jr., at the controls, Gemini nods, turns, and rolls. From within the cabin, Wally peers out at the bulky Agena, suspended at the far end of the darkened chamber and half lit by a shower of artificial sunlight.

"Starting docking maneuver," Wally calls as he nudges the propulsion handle. A low hiss issues from the simulated thrusters. But rather than the Gemini moving, as it would in actual flight, the Agena moves. With gathering momentum, Agena rushes silently toward the Gemini cabin on cushioned slippers of air.

"Oops, a little too much," Wally says, and pulls back on the control handle. Gingerly he maneuvers the target, a silver tube with flickering rendezvous light. There is a slight bump as the vehicles come together.

"It always reminds me of inflight refueling," Wally remarks as he nudges the blunt nose of Gemini into the basketlike adapter ring on the Agena.

"Daddy Longlegs" Teaches Lunar Landings

After mastering the moving-base trainers, the astronaut takes the final examination: simulators that actually fly.

In NASA's Flight Research Center at Edwards Air Force Base, California, the astronauts practice landings in the LLRV—Lunar Landing Research Vehicle. This jet-powered "daddy longlegs" performs here on earth as the LEM will on the moon.

A powerful jet engine, almost hidden in the center of its aluminum skeleton, points constantly downward. With its push, the bizarre craft takes off vertically and ascends to more than 1,000 feet. There the astronaut throws a switch that throttles the engine back to compensate for precisely five-sixths the weight of the vehicle. The remaining weight makes the vehicle fall at just the speed with which it would approach (Continued on page 118)

Clad in hospital white, *John Young (center) and Gus Grissom (right) inspect the adapter ring that will join the pilots' cabin of their Gemini craft with a section containing vital flight equipment. An engineer checks connections to the fuel chamber that powers control rockets. In this Clean Room at the McDonnell plant, air filters trap 95 percent of the atmosphere's microscopic dust.*

© 1965 NASA/National Geographic Image Collection

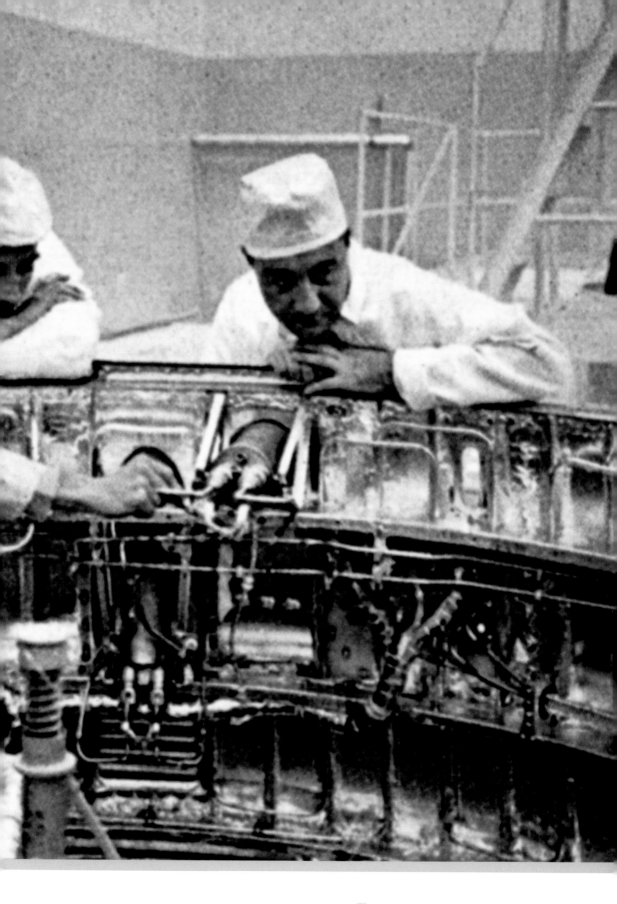

(Continued from page 115) the lunar surface under influence of the moon's weaker gravity.

From this point down, the pilot brakes and maneuvers his craft with small rocket motors like those planned for the LEM.

A practice landing on the desert is as close as you can come to the real thing. A mistake could mean ending up in a pile of scrap metal on the desert floor.

With the many simulators in NASA's inventory, the astronauts agree that there is still no substitute for 20 to 30 hours of actual jet flying each month. Lt. Comdr. Charles Conrad, Jr., sums it up well: "It's easy to sit back in a training device and know that if you do something wrong the instructor will push the reset button and you can try again. But in an airplane you're on your own."

But the astronaut must know more than how to fly a spacecraft. He must also learn to handle his own body in drastically changed environments.

The BETA trainer (for Balanced Extravehicular Training Aircraft) accustoms him to moving about in frictionless space. This metal saucer floats above a steel floor, as if by magic, on cushions of compressed air. A doughnut-shape tank between saucer and floor emits the sustaining air through tiny jets. The astronaut must balance, surfboard style, on the saucer, and with short bursts of air from a multibarreled pistol, he skims across the floor like an Arabian prince on a flying carpet.

A forward-firing burst from the pistol sends the saucer scooting backward; fire to the rear, and the saucer reverses direction. It's the world's lowest-flying aircraft—at one-thousandth of an inch altitude.

"The trick is to shoot from the hip, from the body's center of gravity," BETA inventor Harold I. Johnson points out. "If you hold the gun at eye level, you spin head over heels."

The astronauts experience total or partial weightlessness for just under half a minute in the padded cabin of a modified KC-135 jet tanker as it reaches the peak of a roller-coaster trajectory.

Much of our training comes under the heading 'preparing for the unexpected'.

Lt. Comdr. John W. Young described the sensation as "something like swimming, except that in water you can always get into motion by kicking your feet. Here, with nothing to push against, you just hang there until the plane pulls out of its trajectory."

For Apollo crew training we can also fly the KC-135 in a slightly more shallow parabolic trajectory and produce one-sixth the force of earth gravity. This helps in testing the tools and instruments designed for use on the moon's surface.

Walking on Wall Not Just for Flies

Another device enables the astronaut to move about on earth as he would in the lower gravity of the lunar surface. In this simulator at NASA's Langley Research Center in Virginia, the astronaut hangs in a harness like a puppet and walks flylike on an inclined wall. The angle of the wall is designed so that just one-sixth of his weight rests against it.

Eventually the space voyager must return—and so must his weight. As he hurtles into our resistant atmosphere, he briefly experiences the unpleasant sensation of weighing more than half a ton.

Gemini pilots have conditioned themselves to endure this phenomenon at the U. S. Naval Medical Acceleration Laboratory in Johnsville, Pennsylvania, where they ride a one-man gondola around a circular course at high rates of acceleration.

A larger centrifuge is under construction at the Manned Spacecraft Center. The electric motor, which will propel a three-man gondola simulating the Apollo spacecraft, will be one of the world's largest direct-current motors. The rotor alone will weigh almost 100 tons—twice as much as Apollo's payload!

"Much of our training comes under the heading 'preparing for the unexpected,'" Astronaut Neil A. Armstrong says. "We don't expect to abort, or use our parachutes. Nor do we think we'll ever bring a spacecraft down in the Amazon jungles or the Gobi Desert. Still, we take every step to be ready."

Crew members practice their parachute landings in Galveston Bay. A boat tows the astronaut into the air, a procedure cheaper and easier than using a plane. Starting a few feet back from the water's edge, he allows the breeze to fill the canopy before signaling the helmsman to pour on power. The astronaut launches himself with a few running steps, and his chute lifts him as high as 400 feet. Once aloft he releases the towline and floats down to a wet but safe landing.

Getting wet is nothing new in astronaut training, however. "Until we add some sort of gliding capability and landing gear to our spacecraft, ocean recovery is likely to remain the best way of coming down from orbit," says Lt. Comdr. Alan L. Bean, astronaut specialist in recovery systems. "Those thousands of square miles of uncluttered water surface offer a very handy shock absorber."

At the Naval Air Station in Pensacola, Florida, each crew member learns to swim while encumbered by a bulky pressure suit. The Navy swimming pool is also a good place to learn how to untangle himself from parachute shroud lines, how to use his one-man life raft, and how to get into a helicopter rescue sling.

Actual practice in getting out of the Gemini spacecraft begins in the water test basin at Ellington Air Force Base, here at Houston. Using what we call a "boilerplate" Gemini, intended only for tests or training, a two-man team learns to coordinate body movements with the spacecraft to keep from tipping it over. Similar sessions follow in the open water of nearby Galveston Bay.

Survival "Classrooms": Desert and Jungle

To learn what to do in the punishing sun of the desert, the astronauts travel to Stead Air Force Base in the dry sagebrush country of western Nevada.

Before they are turned loose for two days in the wilderness, the astronauts must learn to make emergency clothes of parachute material: sheik-style headdress and flowing robes of orange and white nylon.

Despite dire tales of sidewinders and Gila monsters, we've had only one small incident to mar the training. John Young was stung on the ankle by a scorpion, but he took care of his own wound, refusing offers of medical help from the base. "After all," he reasoned, "I wouldn't find any medics wandering around in the Sahara."

We've also turned space trainees loose in the tropical rain forests of Panama. At the Air Force Southern Command Tropic Survival School at Albrook Air Force Base in the Canal Zone, the jungle training includes instruction on edible wild fruits and insects—even how to skin and prepare snake meat. Despite initial grimaces, the astronauts found most of the dishes fairly palatable.

"It just depends on your appetite," said Capt. William A. Anders, as he turned down an iguana tidbit. "I've already eaten once this week."

Survival exercises have shown the astronauts to be competent outdoorsmen. Still, it's all pretty uncomfortable, as Alan Bean indicated when I asked what the training had taught him: "I learned that the best thing to do is to try very hard to keep from coming down in the jungle."

We hope our trips to the moon will help determine the origin of the moon and the earth. Therefore our space science training stresses geology.

We begin at the level of a college freshman course. But the dosage is highly concentrated. We soon move on to the most recent ideas about lunar geology.

Our geology classroom at Ellington looks like a small museum of mineral science. The displays combine large globes of the moon and models of lunar terrain. There are sample collections of rocks, meteorites, minerals, and crystals.

Moon Vista May Look Familiar

In addition, two acres of craters are being constructed in the Texas soil by trucking in volcanic rock and cinders—materials that geologists consider similar to what we will find on the moon. A full-size mock-up of the Lunar Excursion Module will squat in this moon-field, so astronauts can test methods for getting in and out. Here, too, they will try out their moonboots, gloves, and scientific gear.

"We will keep improving this piece of the moon as new information comes in from our Ranger and Surveyor programs," said Dr. Ted H. Foss of NASA's special geology team.

Already, from Ranger VII's photographs we have reason to believe that our moonfield does not have to be a deep dustbin. We hope to perfect our simulation to the point that the first astronaut on the moon will say, "Hey, this reminds me of Houston...."

Lunar Hazard: Space Suit Blowout

Field trips give the astronauts a firsthand acquaintance with land forms, rock strata, and the folding, bending forces recorded in layers of stone.

"Grand Canyon makes a magnificent classroom," says geology instructor Uel Clanton. "Several hundred million years of the earth's history sliced into a mile-deep cross section—like a laboratory model blown up to full scale."

In addition to Grand Canyon, astronauts have traveled to the Big Bend country of the Rio Grande and to Arizona's Sunset Crater, where they scrambled over contorted black lava flows.

"If the moon is really volcanic," instructor Al Chidester told them, "you may find yourself trying to walk across this kind of lava field in a pressure suit."

Maj. Frank Borman eyed the glass-sharp edges of the rock heaps. "An embarrassing place to have a flat," he noted. "With a slow leak in your suit you might make it back to the LEM—but with a blowout, you're dead!"

At Kitt Peak National Observatory, Arizona, the astronauts took a look at lunar craters through the world's largest solar telescope

Geologist Dr. Harold Masursky pointed out that few major telescopes are used for moon observation. "The size of the instrument is not too important for moon viewing," he said. "Our atmosphere is the worst problem."

"What *would* be the best optical system for studying the moon?" Bill Anders asked.

Walter Cunningham offered an answer: "A hand-held magnifying glass—you just have to get close enough to use it."

Getting close enough will take a few years. But, as our NASA team works and plans and trains, the moon becomes a bit nearer our grasp with each passing day.

Discussion Questions

- At the time he wrote the article, Dr. Robert R. Gilruth directed NASA's Gemini project. How do you think the article would be different if it were written from the perspective of one of the astronauts who was training for this project?

- Gilruth does, however, include quotes from some of the astronauts. How effective are these quotes in illustrating Gilruth's points?

- Who do you think is the intended audience for this article? Is the author making a point as he provides details about how the astronauts are trained?

- Gilruth includes information on how astronauts are trained to endure difficult physical situations, but he says little about how the astronauts are prepared psychologically for their mission. Why do you think he left this information out of the article?

Writing Activities

- Conduct research on the current state of the space program in the United States. Write an argument about your position on the continuation of the program, outlining whether or not you think the country should continue to fund manned space flights and/or scientific explorations of deep space exploration.

- Conduct research on the first female astronauts. Find out when they became a part of space exploration, whether any training modifications were enacted for them, and how successful they were as astronauts. Write a report of your findings.

- Find information about the Challenger disaster and write an analysis of what caused it.

- Imagine that you are an astronaut living on a space station by yourself for a month. Write a narrative about one day at that station, focusing on how you would cope with the isolation.

Collaborative Activities

- Discuss in your group ways that NASA could get funding to continue its space programs.

- Have the members in your group list all of the movies that they have seen about space travel. Discuss how these films have romanticized these endeavors.